Jaffee

Tavern of the Seas

SUNBIRD PUBLISHING

2 4 6 8 10 9 7 5 3 1
Sunbird Publishing (Pty) Ltd, 34 Sunset Avenue, Llandudno, Cape Town, South Africa
Registration number: 4850177827
Copyright © 2003 published edition: Sunbird Publishing, Copyright © 2003 text: TV Bulpin, Copyright © 2003 photographs: Mark Skinner, except p78 and p102 (left): Dick Wilkins, Vineyard Hotel: p57, Buitenverwachting: p71
Previous edition published by TV Bulpin, 1995
Publisher Dick Wilkins
Editor Peter Joyce
Copy Editor Brian Johnson-Barker
Design concept Peter Bosman
DTP layout Mandy McKay
Production Manager Andrew de Kock
Reproduction by Unifoto (Pty) Ltd, Cape Town. Printed and bound by Tien Wah Press (Pte) Ltd, Singapore
ISBN 062404081X

Previous page Sand, sea and mountain, and a view all the way from Llandudno to Hout Bay, and Noordhoek beyond.
Above Table Mountain and the Waterfront buildings are reflected in the waters of the Victoria Basin.
Opposite The protea family, including Leucospermum cordifolium, flourishes on Table Mountain.

CONTENTS

CHAPTER ONE

THE BIRTH OF A CITY

APE TOWN IS FORTUNATE. There are few other cities so splendidly displayed, so influenced by a benign setting of mountains which, by their presence, sowed its seeds, nurtured its roots, directed its growth and provided it with so handsome a background.

The city and the mountains belong to one another. Cape Town without the mountains would not be quite so interesting. The mountains – Table Mountain, Devil's Peak, Lion's Head and Signal Hill – would still be superb without the city, but their offspring provides them with an animated contrast of capricious moods, an unfolding drama of events, an agreeable mix of sounds, aromas, scandals, all taking place beneath the overlooking piles of rock, like children playing at the feet of indulgent parents.

Look down upon Cape Town from the mountain heights, one of the great views of the world. It is spectacular by day, exquisite by night, especially beautiful in the early evening when a golden glow lingers from the sunset and, one by one, countless lights start to appear like stars descending from the Milky Way to dance and play in the city all night.

STORY OF A MOUNTAIN

How did it all start? As mountains go, Table Mountain is no giant. It is only 1 086 m high but, standing next to the sea, every metre of it is visible. It is one of the most renowned shipping landfalls on Earth. It stands on the southwest end of Africa, its distinctive shape looming up as a gigantic beacon halfway on one of the globe's principal trade-routes, the sea lane around Africa linking east to west.

In making this mountain and positioning it so strategically, nature revealed a piquant sense of humour and sympathy to human needs. Not only was the mountain so positioned as to be seen from far out to sea, but its unique shape made it easily identifiable. To make it even more distinctive, nature provided it with a cloud table-cloth, a phenomenon created by the action of the southeasterly wind, which carries a heavy load of moisture, picked up in its passage over the warm waters of the

Right The Delville Wood memorial in the Gardens commemorates the battle of the Somme in 1916.

Mozambique-Agulhas Current which reaches the end of its flow in False Bay. Orographic condensation turns this moisture into cloud as the wind is forced to rise over the mountain top and suddenly cools. Tumbling over the northern edge of the tabletop, the wind falls immediately back to a lower and warmer level. The cloud disappears at this level and Table Mountain is left with its table-cloth.

Who were the first human beings to see the majestic spectacle of Table Mountain and its cloud? Fossils and artefacts at least 15 000 years old have been found in caves in the Cape Peninsula. Until recently examples of rock art on the walls of cave shelters on Table Mountain itself were reminders, until they faded away, of the presence in former years of people of the Later Stone Age.

Legends tell that Phoenician and Arab sailors, 2 000 and more years ago, were the first to reach the mountain from the sea. The Phoenicians, circumnavigating Africa for the first time from Europe, are said to have landed at the foot of the mountain to rest, repair their ships, and replenish their food by planting and reaping crops of wheat. The Arab sailors, exploring the east coast of Africa, described Table Mountain as a magic place, with a magnetism which drew ships to doom.

The Phoenicians were looking for a way around the southern end of the African continent; the Arabs more particularly for an extension of their slave, ivory and gold trading enterprises on the east coast. To both the pioneer groups and the countless seafarers who followed them, Table Mountain became the eagerly looked-for beacon at the end of Africa. Fresh water could always be obtained there from the mountain streams. Meat could be bartered from the nomadic pastoral people of unknown name who grazed their herds in the area.

A MEETING OF CULTURES

It is not known who were the first of the modern European seafarers to see Table Mountain and its bay. The records of the discovery of the Cape of Good Hope by Bartholomeu Dias in 1488 are incomplete and make no mention of it.

The written story started in 1503 when the Portuguese admiral, António de Saldanha, on his way to the East with a fleet of three ships, mislaid his position and found himself quite inadvertently sailing into Table Bay. After anchoring, Saldanha left his men on the shore to replenish water casks while he and a party followed the freshwater stream to the foot of the mountain and then up the Platteklip Gorge, which provides the only relatively easy climb to the summit. From the top he could see the whole of the Cape Peninsula as far as the Cape of Good Hope, and this grand view of the classic peninsula shape cleared the confusion in his mind about his whereabouts.

Back on the shore, Saldanha found his men trying to bargain for livestock with the resident pastoral people. The discord of two completely different languages made such bargaining extremely difficult. The haggling deteriorated into a squabble. The first recorded encounter of African and

Opposite The Victoria and Alfred Waterfront is a busy, working harbour as well as a place of recreation.

European on the site of the future city of Cape Town ended in bloodshed. António de Saldanha was slightly wounded himself. The Portuguese were driven back to their ship and they sailed off in disgruntled mood.

From thence on the bay was known to the Portuguese as the Aguada de António de Saldanha ('Watering place of António de Saldanha). Seven years later Dom Francisco de Almeida, returning to Portugal after a bloody five year spell as the first Portuguese Viceroy of India, put into Table Bay with a fleet of three ships. The crew replenished drinking water from the mountain stream and started a trade for livestock with a group of pastoralists somewhere on the site of the present suburb of Woodstock. Everything seemed to be going well, with the Africans friendly, killing a sheep and inviting the Portuguese to a feast.

Then a fight developed - for obscure reasons, but said to have begun when the Portuguese attempted to take a man by force either as a hostage or to meet their commander. The language barrier was impenetrable. The Portuguese were driven to the beach. Almeida decided that the prestige of Portugal demanded retaliation. A few days later he landed on the beach with 150 men and marched to the African village. In a sur-

prise attack the Portuguese seized a number of children and cattle. There were only about 80 African males but they rallied to rescue their children and livestock. Sheltering behind bullocks trained for combat, they charged at the Portuguese, throwing stones and spears in a barrage. It was the turn of the Portuguese to be surprised. They retreated to the beach and were dismayed to find that the sailors who had conveyed them from the anchored ships had moved further eastwards.

There was a running battle as the Portuguese, many of them already wounded, retreated along the beach. Reinforcements reached the Africans, and now 170 men harassed the heavily armed Portuguese. Almeida died with a spear through his throat. Seventy-five of his men, including eleven officers, died with him. The fact that 170 primitive African people could so overwhelm 150 well-armed European soldiers was considered to be one of the worst disasters in Portuguese history, especially as several of the casualties were members of illustrious families and Almeida was a nobleman of high rank. Few Portuguese ships ventured into the bay at the foot of Table Mountain after this disaster.

ISLAND OF SEALS

Towards the end of the 16th century, seafarers of other nations started to sail around the Cape and they had no qualms in visiting the watering place

of Saldanha. In 1591 the English admiral, George Raymond, with James (later Sir James) Lancaster as captain of one of his three ships, sailed into the bay in search of fresh water and meat. The Englishmen traded as many animals as they wanted – two knives for an ox and one knife for a sheep were considered to be fair prices.

Raymond also sailed over to the kidney-shaped island in the bay, known today as Robben Island ('Island of seals'), where he found an unexpected bounty. There were so many sea birds, eggs and seals that the seafarers recorded that 'there can be no other island in all the world as full of fowl and seal as this. It is astounding'. The Englishmen replenished their food-store and sailed on, leaving behind on the island a number of sheep which were too thin and sickly to withstand a voyage.

From the earliest days Robben Island – just 3,5 km long, 2 km wide – played a peculiarly important role in the story of Cape Town. This importance derived from three characteristics: its strategic position commanding the entrance to Table Bay; its isolation and thus its immunity from mainland predators, and thirdly its shales and deposits of marine shells (limestone), both valuable building materials, and its wildlife – penguins and other sea birds nested on the place in prodigious numbers while seals lolled around completely tame and still to learn of man's rapacity.

Dutch sailors also made considerable use of Robben Island. In 1601 Joris van Spilbergen named it *Cornelia* after his mother. He had visited Dassen Island as he came down the west coast and named it *Elizabeth*. On that odd island he had been surprised, as all visitors have been, at the presence of the dassies (coneys) which have given the island its name. The origin of these little animals on an island so isolated from the mainland (where they are common) would have slightly puzzled Charles Darwin. Captain Van Spilbergen captured a number of them for food and released a few on his Cornelia Island as some exchange for the plump sheep which he found there, now running wild.

Leaving some surplus livestock on Robben Island to fatten in safety, and then be replaced in exchange with thinner animals by later voyagers, became a courteous habit no matter whether the seafarers were friends or enemies. Another habit which started at this time, on both the island and the mainland, was to inscribe stones with the name of a ship and the date of its visit. Underneath these stones letters were placed with requests that they be carried forward, east or west as required, by other ships. The courtesy was granted even in times of war. The so-called 'Post-Office Stones' became a custom of visitors to Table Bay and those letters which survive tell engrossing stories of sea fights, storms, wrecks, adventures, hopes, disappointments and the hardship of long voyages in

itors overcame the difficulty by applying a nickname to the pastoralists, Hottentot, said by some to mean a stammerer, from the odd sounds in their speech and by others to have originated from a rhythmic word sounding like *huttentutton*, which the pastoralists are said to have repeated constantly while they danced. The smaller and less numerous hunter-gatherer people were eventually given by the Dutch the name of Bosjesmans (Bushmen) because they seemed to lurk in the cover of the shrubs. The pastoralists referred offhandedly to these people as *Sonkwa*. The origin and ancestral relationship of the hunter-gatherers and the pastoralists remains unknown. Their languages were similar but their lifestyles very different. They were both, however, essentially nomadic, wandering about in groups or small tribes, each group having its own name and not recognising any paramount power or generic name.

The seafarers had some peculiar ideas of winning friends and influencing the local inhabitants. They couldn't have had it much better. Scrap metal and junk trinkets bartered for enough fat slaughter animals to provision one whole fleet; 39 fat oxen and 115 sheep in exchange for 'a little brass which we cut from two or three old kettles'. This was in 1612.

The English felt that things could be still better if they had a resident middleman who could ensure trade. To this purpose, in 1613, the chief of the local pastoralists (whose name sounded like Cory), together with another man, was lured on board a homeward-bound ship and kidnapped. One man died on the voyage but Cory reached England, where the plan was to teach him English and for the company to learn from him something of the possibilities of the Cape country for trade. Cory was even dressed in clothes of the current English fashion. He was accommodated in London in the home of Sir Thomas Smythe, the founder of the English East India Company. He would lie on the ground crying and pleading 'Cory home go, Souldana go, home go', over and over.

Smythe eventually relented and sent Cory back to the Cape. As soon as he landed he bolted for home, tore off his English clothing and reverted to traditional dress. The English were disgruntled. They complained that the bottom line bargaining price for livestock went up sharply after Cory's return, although it was still cheap enough.

THE DEEP DIVIDE

It was on the shores of Table Bay that, at this time, a development was taking place with consequences which were to bedevil the whole turbulent story of Southern Africa. A plural society was being spawned from complete misunderstanding between persons of African and non-African origin. The division was not caused so much by colour, as by a barrier of

---

appalling conditions, with bad water, worse food, dismal living conditions, and the ships haunted by the dreadful curse of scurvy, 'a disease which rots the flesh and makes the mouth like an open sore'.

NAMES AND NICKNAMES

With the launching in 1600 of the English East India Company and in 1602 of the Dutch East India Company there was a considerable increase of shipping calling in Table Bay. Only the Portuguese continued to bypass the Cape, using as their refreshment place the islet of Mozambique, 3 000 km further north.

The Cape was extolled by nearly all the English and Dutch seafarers who called there. It was halfway on what could be a terrible journey. The climate was healthy, the water from the Fresh River (as it was called) tasted exquisitely pure and sweet. There was no malarial fever; and, as Thomas Aldworth, senior merchant for the English East India Company reported to his superiors, he arrived there 'with many of our people sick, they all regained their health and strength within twenty days'. As for the local pastoralists, Aldworth found 'the natives of the country to be very courteous and tractable folk, and they did not give us the least annoyance during the time we were there'.

Nobody knew what to call these indigenous African inhabitants. The clicks and odd sounds in their language made it extremely difficult for visitors to understand them or pronounce any word or name. The Dutch vis-

Above The Foreshore area was under water until the 1930's, when a land reclamation scheme was commenced.

Opposite Cape Town city centre and Table Bay, seen from Tafelberg Road on Table Mountain.

separate cultures and languages, each with sounds extremely difficult for the other group to learn or pronounce. The two divisions in the Cape simply could not communicate or comprehend each other's life-style or ethos. They had to formulate assessments of each other by superficial observation during casual encounters.

To the Africans, seafarers of whatever origin, Asian or European, were, at first, just curiosities and no threat because they did not stay long. But as traders they were demanding – and it was inevitable that the rubbish they offered for livestock would soon become unacceptable. The newcomers' obvious disdain of the African's clothing, eating habits and hygiene was irritating. African clothing suited the climate and was the product of available dress materials. Their eating habits were to the taste of the Africans and, as for hygiene, the rancid fat they rubbed into their bodies might stink to the visitors but it drove away bugs. It was the visitors who looked sick near to death when they arrived, recovered in the healthy environment and then sailed away leaving behind such scourges as the smallpox and venereal disease which caused heavy mortality to the indigenous people.

As for culture, the Africans had their music, traditions, legends and religion. The seafarers considered them to be barbarians with no schools or buildings better than huts, no signs of parliament, government, tax collections, churches or the evident signs of religion in the form of vestments, ceremonies, services, attendance registers and promises of rewards to come in another world. The Africans were bemused by this; they had not much belief in paradise to come and soon discovered the fact, particularly important for them, that none of the foreign religions had the least condemnation of slavery. The Ten Commandments and the golden rule of not doing to others that which you would not have them do to you were indeed preached but definitely not much practised. The vaunted superiority of Eastern and Western civilisations, to the Africans, amounted to nothing against the barbarous murders, wars, inhumanity and ruthless exploitation of the environment, which were so integral a part of the lifestyle of the newcomers.

Finally, there was the matter of land. The visitors saw no sign of fences, cultivation or private ownership. The African concept of collective ownership was completely contrary to the ideas of European and Asian people. Private property, to them, was sacrosanct, but here, beneath Table Mountain, there was no sign of any such thing. The whole land seemed to be wide open, up for the taking.

COLONIAL OVERTURE

Notwithstanding their disappointment in Cory, the director of the English East India Company decided on establishing a permanent presence at the Cape. His method of effecting this presence was rather peculiar. From King James I he obtained a reprieve for seventeen condemned prisoners, who were offered the choice of the gallows or the Cape. With some hesitation they accepted the Cape. They were joined voluntarily by three other convicts. On 5 June 1615, Cory and his people were somewhat disconcerted to see landed on the shores of Table Bay nine of these felons led by a celebrated highwayman and former yeoman of the Royal Guard known as Captain James Crosse. This little band was supposed to start a plantation, be grateful to their king for saving their lives, behave like Christians, and explore the country to see if they could discover anything which might be beneficial to England and to their honourable employers.

The means given to the men to enable them to effect these miracles were pitiful: a tent, some turnip seeds and spades, two knives, a short pike, a sword and a knapsack for each man, a store of bread, dried Newfoundland fish and, as an act of charity, a little wine and 'strong water'. They also had use of a ship's whaleboat, which allowed them to make their base in security on Robben Island. The idea was to stock the island with livestock bartered from the mainland pastoralists. Visiting ships could be provided with a dependable supply of fresh meat.

The idea was interesting but, in view if the type of men involved, it never had a real chance. The islanders found additional interests on the mainland, and Captain Crosse had his throat slit in a quarrel over women. The whaleboat was wrecked on the island's rocky coast and the men were marooned. After eight months, a ship was seen on the horizon but seemed to have no intention of venturing into Table Bay. The islanders, by then, were 'almost mad by reason of their several pressing wants and extremities'. They had made a raft from the wreckage of the whaleboat. On this, four of the men attempted to paddle to the ship. They were overturned in a swell and drowned.

The next day the ship, homeward-bound to England, entered Table Bay. The surviving islanders begged to be taken away. Within a few hours of landing in England, the three were arrested for stealing a purse. They were hanged by special warrant of the Lord Chief Justice who, without further trial, simply revived their original condemnation.

On 3 July 1620 two English commanders, Commodore Andrew Shillinge and Captain Humphrey Fitzherbert, annexed the Cape to King James, hoisted the flag of St George and erected a cairn of stones on what they called 'King James his Mount' (now Signal Hill).

Nothing resulted from this annexation. The English government and the East India Company were on friendly terms with the Dutch and quite happy to let them have the Cape if they wanted it.

Meanwhile, Cory had died and the English visitors tried to find a replacement middleman. About 1631 one of their ships bound for the East took aboard a beachcomber who they named Harry. He was given a round trip, taught some English on the journey, well treated, and returned safely to Table Bay. Unfortunately he was not esteemed by the pastoral tribes. He and his people were lowly *strandlopers* (beachcombers, so named by the Dutch) who lived largely on dead whales and the sea creatures washed up on shore. The superior pastoral people would have none of him.

To save Harry from being killed, the English removed him and a number of his clan to Robben Island where they could live safely, and where Harry could continue his career as interpreter and negotiator. Some such arrangement was very needful. In March 1632, just before Harry returned to the Cape, 23 of the crew of a Dutch ship had been killed when, it is said, they tried to seize cattle without payment to the owners.

THE HAPPY CASTAWAYS

Notwithstanding such disasters, the reputation of the Cape as a place of refreshment grew. In 1647 this reputation received a considerable boost. On 25 March of that year the homeward-bound Dutch ship *Haarlem* had the misfortune of being blown by a southeast gale on to the beach at Blouberg on the northern end of Table Bay. Nobody was drowned but the ship stuck fast and it was carrying a valuable cargo. Most of the crew and passengers were taken aboard two other Dutch ships anchored in the bay, while 40 others were given passage to Europe aboard two English ships. The 60 men who remained, led by a junior merchant, Leendert Janssen, stayed to salvage the cargo. They built a small fort on shore and, in the months they stayed there, worked, planted a vegetable garden, fished, hunted and rowed over to Robben Island to gather penguins, eggs and to club seals to secure oil for their lamps.

A few beachcombers were the only local inhabitants they at first encountered, but after five months a group of pastoralists wandered into the area and were quite happy to trade cattle and sheep for what they considered to be fair exchange in items from the shipwreck. The shipwrecked men lived well and were even able to supply meat and vegetables to ships that called. In March 1648 a homeward-bound fleet of twelve Dutch ships arrived. The salvaged cargo, 60 healthy men and ample stocks of food were taken aboard and conveyed in good order to the Netherlands. The report compiled by Janssen and Nicolaas Proot, a fellow member of the shipwrecked party, to the Dutch East India Company eulogised the Cape, its health, peaceful inhabitants, and possibilities of profit from seals, whales, fishing, and supplying food to passing ships. As a consequence of this report, the Company, on 20 March 1651, finally decided to establish a victualling station at the Cape. It was a momentous decision for Southern Africa.

Two ships, *Dromedaris* and *Reiger*, and a yacht *Goede Hoop* were commissioned to convey to the Cape a party of 70 men. The command was offered to Nicolaas Proot. When he declined the position, it was offered to 33-year-old Johan (Jan) van Riebeeck, who had already seen

Above The reconstructed Dolphin Pool within the Castle courtyard, much as it was in Lady Anne's time.

service in the East with the Company as an under-surgeon and then as assistant clerk. After some trouble over private trading at Tonkin he had been recalled to Holland in 1648. He left the Company, married Maria Quevellerius (also known as Maria de la Queillerie), made trading voyages to Greenland and the West Indies and then rejoined the Company with the rank of merchant at the pay of £4. 11s. 8d a month. He accepted the offer to lead the venture to the Cape.

On his first return voyage from the East, Van Riebeeck had lived on shore at the Cape for three weeks while the cargo of the wrecked *Haarlem* was being loaded on the homeward-bound ships. He shared the opinion that the Cape was suitable for a permanent refreshment station.

THE FIRST SETTLERS

The instructions given to Van Riebeeck and the captains of the three ships were to proceed directly to Table Bay. The materials for a wooden building were included in the loading of the ships and, on arrival, this was to be erected close to the all-important watering place at the mouth of the Fresh River. A site for a fort had then to be selected and the stronghold built as quickly as possible. It was designed to accommodate about 80

men. Four small cannon of the type known as culverins were to be mounted on the fort's angles. Once secure in this fort, Van Riebeeck and his men had to take possession of a fertile extent of arable land suitable for vegetable and fruit cultivation. A professional gardener, Hendrik Boom and his family, were members of Van Riebeeck's party.

The party was instructed not to injure any of the local inhabitants or their cattle but to endeavour to win friendship. The instruction did not indicate how this goodwill could be obtained and maintained if select sites for occupation, agriculture and grazing were also to be set up without negotiation or suggested payment. All nations except Portugal would be welcome to trade and even to occupy areas of the country for themselves beyond the Company's boundaries.

On Sunday, 24 December 1651, a fine easterly wind blew from the mainland of Europe. Like a flock of birds waiting to migrate, a whole fleet of Dutch merchant ships set sail for many far ports of trade. Amongst these vessels were the two ships and the yacht *Goede Hoop* conveying Van Riebeeck and his party to the Cape. The voyage was uneventful and, for those days, speedy, and on 5 April 1652, about the fifth glass of the afternoon watch, the chief mate of the *Dromedaris* saw Table Mountain rise just above the horizon.

Captain Coninck of the *Dromedaris* was the first to go ashore with six armed soldiers and a party of sailors. They landed just after dawn, caught delicious fish in a seine net, collected some herbs and found a box containing three letters left on 26 February by the admiral of a homeward-bound fleet. Later that afternoon, Van Riebeeck went ashore with a party to select the best site for the fort.

The area of the future city of Cape Town had been well dehydrated by the summer season of the southeast wind. Wildlife as well as the pastoralists had abandoned the place until the winter rains came to refresh it. In a swamp close to the present Church Square, a few hippos garumphed at the intruders. The only human inhabitants were Harry and his clan of beachcombers. Van Riebeeck learned that Harry's people, a very small clan, had a name which the Dutch wrote as 'Goringhaikona', the nearest they could get to recording the clicks and exotic sounds. Two larger clans of pastoralists habitually used the area for grazing when the rains came. They were the (Dutch spelling) Goringhaikwa and the Gorachoukwa. At least eight other pastoral clans had their grazing areas in what is now the province of the Western Cape. All these clans were nomadic, wandering about in search of the best grazing. They were generally peaceful, the country was large and there were not many of them. They could avoid one another. These were the people nicknamed Hottentots by the Dutch. They had no generic name for themselves.

Work started the next day, 8 April, on erecting a wooden house and store shed close to the mouth of the Fresh River. The site for the fort was selected where the fruit stalls stand today on what is known as the Grand Parade in the centre of modern Cape Town. One hundred men were selected from the three vessels to work on construction on shore and were housed in tents.

On 24 April, Van Riebeeck and his family removed from the *Dromedaris* to the shore. On the previous evening a hippopotamus had been killed in the swamp and on this animal the whole party feasted. They likened the flesh to veal and craved for more, but hippos were difficult to kill with the muskets and balls of the period. For some time the principal items on the Cape menu were the fish which swarmed in huge shoals in Table Bay and were described by Van Riebeeck and his people as the most delicious they had ever tasted. These fish made a hard, cold, wet, miserable winter bearable. Everything else was in short supply.

There was, though, a silver lining: the rains transformed the vegetation and softened the soil. Hendrik Boom, the gardener, made haste to plant seeds and soon health-restoring vegetables were growing. Great herds of game animals also appeared in the area on what was apparently their seasonal migration. The sight of these wild animals made the longing for fresh meat almost an obsession but the inexperienced hunters had little success with their simple weapons. In the whole winter season, only one young hartebeest was run down by dogs. For the rest, the wild animals outwitted marksmen, traps and pitfalls with agile impunity.

Van Riebeeck looked to Robben Island for a solution, for that little place always seemed to be productive of something interesting. The yacht was sent over and came back with over 100 carcasses of sea birds and 3 000 penguin eggs, a very welcome addition to food supplies. He also decided it was time to examine the possibilities of the country behind Devil's Peak. This beautiful and fertile agricultural land delighted him. He thought that if a population of Chinese settlers could be introduced to farm this area (now known as Constantia) an unlimited supply of vegetables and other produce could be obtained for supply to shipping. But nothing came of the scheme. Hendrik Boom, the gardener, was left with the assistance of a few labourers supplied from the garrison to slowly create the Company's vegetable garden close to the fort.

Living conditions in the primitive fort were miserable. The feeling of isolation and insecurity made the men quarrelsome and insubordinate. Many would have deserted if there was any place where they could go. Discipline in the fort was severe, while outside there was a vast continent filled with unimaginable dangers. Lions seemed to be crowding around the fort, even attempting to assault the place.'This night,' wrote Van Riebeeck 'it appeared as if the lions would take the fort by storm, that they might get at the sheep, they made a fearful noise, as if they would destroy all within but they could not climb the walls ...'

THE COMING OF THE CAPE PEOPLE

The annual migration of the Goringhaikwa people to the Cape, with their flocks and herds, took place at the beginning of October. On the 9th of the month two of their men arrived at the fort. They were far stronger looking than the beachcombers of Harry. They were armed with spears and sticks, naked except for a well-prepared skin draped down over one of their arms as European gallants affected a mantle. Their arms and legs were decorated with ivory and copper ornaments. They were friendly, informed Van Riebeeck that their people would soon be coming to graze their livestock on the spring growth of fresh grass and herbs. Van Riebeeck was delighted. He showed them his stock of trade goods – copper, brass and other metals, tobacco and alcohol, gave them samples and entertained them hospitably before they returned to their people. The rest of the Gorinkhaikwa arrived a few days later and camped on the sites of the future suburbs of Rondebosch and Claremont. Harry acted as interpreter, assisted by his niece, a bright child of about 11 years who was named Eva by the Europeans. She took up residence in the fort, was taught Dutch, Christianity, assorted European skills and industry and dressed like a young lady from Holland. The pastoral tribes were becoming known to Van Riebeeck and his party by the colloquial name of 'Kaapmans' ('Cape people'), abbreviated at times to Capeys.

Not all went according to plan, though. Through the interpreters, Harry and his young niece, the Cape people repeatedly asked when the English were coming. They were reluctant to part with any large numbers of their livestock. The settlers became aggrieved and thought that Harry had somehow prejudiced the Cape People against the Dutch because they had settled permanently on the traditional grazing grounds of the tribe. Van Riebeeck candidly recorded his thoughts in his diary: 'What would it

Above Some 6 000 plant species, including proteas, flourish on the Peninsula mountains.

matter if we took at once from them 6 000 or 8 000 cattle, there is opportunity enough for it, as we do not perceive that they are very strong in number, but indeed very timorous, coming often only two or three men driving 1 000 cattle under our guns.' The directors in the Netherlands, however, prohibited such action.

Meanwhile, visitors to the Cape were captivated by the scenery and the lovely flora of one of the Earth's principal domains of wild flowers. It was a vast natural garden in a superb scenic setting. As the intended Tavern of the Sea expanded its facilities and reputation for hospitality so visitors would be attracted, if not to settle, then at least to see so remarkable a place. The first stirrings of a future tourist industry were taking place.

ANXIOUS TIMES

Restraints by the parent authority in Europe on the headstrong doings of its colonial offspring were destined to become increasingly contentious as the years passed. Van Riebeeck'd superiors, however, approved at least

one of his urgent desires – his demand for labour. The Cape people were not much tempted into work for the newcomers. Nor were they physically suited to slavery, and they would find it too easy to run away. Imported slaves were regarded as the answer. The Cape settlement therefore became one more market for slave traders to dispose of their wares. The slaves came mainly from the nearest source of supply, Angola, and they supplied the human material for the system of forced labour management which was considered to be normal in the world at that time.

These were anxious days for Van Riebeeck. On 18 January 1653, the galiot *Zwarte Vos* arrived with the news that war had broken out between the Netherlands and the Commonwealth of England under Oliver Cromwell. This was very bad news. The Netherlands was already at war with Portugal and Van Riebeeck in his fort had little defence against any attack by either of the hostile maritime powers. The fort was just about capable of keeping at bay the marauding lions and leopards, the available cannon were feeble and, to worsen matters, the local pastoral people were increasingly resentful of the Netherlanders' occupation of the grazing lands. Even Harry and his beachcombers with young Eva sneaked away one day while the garrison was in church, stole 42 of the herd of 44 cattle then in the possession of the Company and murdered the young Dutch herdsman. For the European settlers, times were hard and the future looked bleak.

But ships continued to call for supplies. The vegetable garden was increasingly productive. If beef was in short supply, then penguins and their eggs from the islands provided good eating and the sheep on Robben Island fattened in security.

The anniversary (6 April) of the arrival of Van Riebeeck and his party in the Cape was treated as a day of thanksgiving. At that date there was not much to give thanks for but four months later, with the spring flowers blossoming, there was a change for the better. On 15 August the yacht *Vlieland* arrived with the good news from the Netherlands that there was peace with the English. The oppressive sense of threat and isolation, which had gathered over the settlement, simply vanished away like the storm clouds of winter. International shipping returned to Table Bay, one of the ships bringing the first vine stocks all the way from the vineyards of the Rhine. The indefatigable gardener, Hendrik Boom, soon had them settled in the local soil along with a varied collection of fruit trees and the flourishing fields of vegetables. To the visiting ships, some with more than half of their crew dead or half dead from scurvy, Van Riebeeck's garden, orchard and vineyard at the Cape offered a new chance of life, a little cheer and the beginning of what became the famed cuisine of the Cape.

Cape Classic Cuisine, as it is called, is based on the essential foundation of fresh, tasty local produce, a good contribution from the vineyards and a subtlety of cookery which came from the blending of the skills of Europe, Africa and the East. The Dutch had acquired a liking in Indonesia

for the exotic tastes of that country. These tastes were brought to the Cape to an increasing extent from 1654 onwards. It was in that year that four Indonesians were sentenced by the Dutch court of justice in Batavia to banishment, and hard labour for life. Their crime was resistance to Dutch seizure of their homeland. Three of the men were left on the island of Mauritius. The fourth was landed at the Cape. He was the first of many people to be banished from the East to spend their lives in Southern Africa. Most were from Indonesia; nearly, but not all, were Muslims. For some reason they were indiscriminately known in the Cape as Malays. Their influence on cooking, architecture, building and industry became notable in the story of the Cape.

DOING DEALS WITH THE BLACK CAPTAIN

Trading conditions at the fort improved suddenly in June 1655 when Harry the prodigal reappeared, accompanied by 50 strangers who brought 40 cattle for trade. Harry flatly denied having anything to do with the recent murder and theft of cattle. Van Riebeeck considered it wise to at least pretend to believe the man. Harry even volunteered to lead a party to the shores of False Bay in search of people prepared to trade their cattle. Particularly gratifying was the arrival of a large group of pastoralists under a chief named Gonnema, nicknamed the Black Captain because he used soot as a facial cosmetic instead of the red clay favoured by the Cape people. The newcomers built on the site of the future suburb of Rondebosch an encampment of two hundred huts, linked with a palisade and containing a huge corral (or 'kraal') in which they secured their livestock at night. Van Riebeeck had the satisfaction of trading copper scrap for nearly 400 head of cattle and about the same quantity of sheep. The sheep were taken over to Robben Island for fattening in safety.

Two other local men did duty as interpreters, a beachcomber known as Klaus Das because he had learned Dutch working with the seal hunters on Dassen Island, and a Cape man nicknamed Doman because his demeanour seemed as grave and transparent as a dominee (parson). He was so highly regarded that Van Riebeeck sent him on a round trip to Batavia to expand his knowledge of the Dutch and their language. He returned two years later not quite as angelic as he had seemed when he left the Cape, as will be seen later in this story.

PUTTING DOWN ROOTS

A momentous change to the nature of the Cape settlement came that same year (1655). The directors in Holland revised their plan to have Company employees stationed in what was intended as a simple trading

Left A family celebration in a cosy Bo-Kaap homestead. Bo-Kaap is sometimes known as the Malay Quarter.

station. They decided that employees on completion of their service contracts in the Cape, if they did not wish to return to Europe or be posted to the East, could be settled as freemen on ground close to the fort and earn a living by producing food or by some other industry.

With this decision, the Cape became a colony rather than just a service station on the East-West route.

The directors of the Dutch East India Company unfortunately had much to learn about the peculiar nature of a colony. Their hope was to see the transplant into new soil of the same industrious peasantry that farmed smallholdings in Holland. They failed to appreciate that the contagious cancer of slavery persuaded a 'freeman' or 'free burgher' to take others into bondage, to become a squire, patron or slave master rather than a worker himself. Work was for slaves; the landowner automatically became a gentleperson in the local social scale, craving ever larger land holdings as the means to rise still higher in popular esteem, clamouring for more slave workers whose labour would reward the master with the profits to support an ever more demanding lifestyle.

The facilities offered to shipping were improved in 1656 with the opening of a hospital. A strong wooden jetty was also completed and this was a great convenience to the loading of fresh water casks and general supplies. The first two inns were also opened, one by the wife of Sergeant van Harwarden, the other by Annetje de Boerin, wife of the gardener Hendrik Boom, an enterprising lady who already had secured the right to lease the company-owned herd of dairy cows and supply the community with fresh milk. Industrious Annetjie also raised eight children, and the pioneer family eventually returned to the Netherlands.

Four years after its establishment, the Cape settlement, transforming to a colony, presented a bustling scene. Practically every garden crop of that age was flourishing. Only potatoes and maize had still to be successfully introduced. The genius and industry of Hendrik Boom had created a garden so productive that it now even provided luxuries such as strawberries and blackberries and all things in such quantity that an export business to Batavia of high quality seeds had commenced. Oak and fir trees had been introduced; domestic livestock were flourishing, the wild animals were being driven away by professional hunters and the quality of their venison was much appreciated as an alternative to the meat of domestic animals.

Wheat and barley at first proved difficult to cultivate, for their ripening time unfortunately coincided with the season of the desiccating southeasterly wind. Crops simply withered. Van Riebeeck then discovered that the southeaster was not nearly so venomous on the western side of

Opposite Groote Schuur, once a barn, was the home of Cecil Rhodes and also a prime-ministerial residence.

Bosbergen, along the summit ridge of the Bosheuwel ('Bushy slopes'), below the cluster of granite boulders known from their shape as the Hen and Chickens, and across the flatlands to the mouth of the Salt River. It took some time for this defensive scheme to mature.

The first two groups of freemen, five in one group and four in the second, chose land for themselves on the outer side of the Liesbeek River. They were each gifted by the company with plots about 28 acres (or 13 morgen) in extent and were free of the burden of taxes for twelve years. The prospects looked good. More men decided to take their freedom in the Cape from company service and become property or business owners at no cost to themselves. Not all wanted to be farmers. Wouter Mostert had been a miller in the Netherlands. He set up a water-mill in the upper reaches of the Fresh River. Others became carpenters, tailors, wagonmakers, fishermen, hunters or innkeepers. A straggling little town started to grow in the afternoon shadow of Table Mountain.

PRISON ISLAND

Robben Island also gained in importance. On its highest point a pole, and later a platform, was erected on which pitch rings were set alight each night as a navigational beacon. The hill was named Vuurberg ('Fire mountain') and this was, in its simple way, the first lighthouse on the coast of Southern Africa.

Van Riebeeck found still another use for the island. It was a very handy place to have right on the doorstep of the Cape settlement. All manner of problem human beings could be sent to it and there accommodated well concealed from public view. Van Riebeeck was convinced at that time that Harry the interpreter was playing a treacherous game, pretending friendship but plotting with the Cape people to destroy the settlement before it entirely enveloped their traditional grazing fields. He considered Harry, as interpreter, was now expendable. If Europeans found it almost impossible to learn the local language with its clicks and exotic sounds, some of the Cape people found it relatively far easier to learn Dutch in the form of a local version which started to develop as a convenient medium of communication. People such as Doman and the girl Eva could take over duties of interpretation and negotiation. If Robben Island was difficult to reach for people who had no boats then it would obviously be just as difficult for boatless people to leave. The stone quarries and lime-making industries on the island provided ideal hard labour employment for prisoners.

Accordingly, as Van Riebeeck cynically noted in his diary (July 1658), 'The ex-interpreter, or as the English call him, King Harry, was removed in a sheep boat out of his kingdom in this furthest corner of Africa to Robben Island with two of his companions'. These three Cape men, with some political prisoners exiled in chains from Batavia, were the first to obtain what Van Riebeeck considered secure quarters where the massed arum lilies wave so freely in the wind on Robben Island. The irrepressible Harry, however, was to prove Van Riebeeck wrong – he was the first prisoner to escape from Robben Island. Very few other prisoners had the same audacity and good fortune in the years to follow.

RUMOUR, GREED AND SLAVERY

Life in the infant Cape Town might have been on the rough side but it was certainly eventful and a place of interesting rumours. The legendary land of Monomotapa, the golden Ophir of Solomon and Sheba, was reported to be within easy reach to the north. Friendly cattle-rich tribes were said to live just beyond the mountains. Parties set off in search of this wealth.

No quick wealth in gold or cattle rewarded these explorers. News of their travels, however, fascinated the stay-at-homes in the Cape settlement and provided relief from the continuous rumours of attack from the dispossessed original inhabitants. Eva, the young lady interpreter, was a great source of such assorted tales of riches and troubles to come. She treated listeners to elaborate accounts of the Nama people who she said had white skins, long hair, wore clothing and owned black slaves who tilled the soil, worked mines and built stone houses for their masters. Such tales of gentlemanly living in Africa were beguiling to employees of the Dutch Company. These people of various nationalities had a background in Europe of hard living and poorly rewarded labour. It seemed to them that by being posted for duty to the southwesterly end of Africa, they had escaped from a humdrum existence into a new era of prosperity, of generous land grants, the award of monopolies in trading and professional occupation, of rights to own slaves, of the whole prospect ahead of them of a fat-cat society.

They were all transformed into land owners and moneygrubbers, wanting only lawyers, stock exchange manipulators, developers, promoters, usurers, speculators and swindlers to complete the social strata of the Cape. Even Van Riebeeck was in the real estate business. He was granted land on the southeastern side of the Liesbeek River, and here he planted grapevines, naming the place Wynberg ('Wine mountain'). The name was later transferred to adjoining high ground and Van Riebeeck's farm was renamed Boscheuwel ('Bushy slopes').

The basic contradictions of a slave-based society became apparent when the first substantial number of slaves reached the Cape. On 28 March 1658, the *Amersfoort* brought 170 black Africans to the Cape. On the way from Holland, the *Amersfoort* had captured a Portuguese ship bound from Angola to Brazil with over 500 slaves. The ship was too

Devil's Peak. An experimental crop was grown in the area known as Ronde Doorn Bossien, from a round grove of thorn trees which grew there. The results were excellent. Rondebosch, as the area came to be known, was developed as a wheat farm. A substantial building, known as the Groote Schuur ('Great barn'), was erected to store the grain, as well as a redoubt to shelter a small guard of soldiers.

The whole question of the security of the expanding settlement, especially now that families, under the freeman scheme, would be granted land beyond the protection of the fort, was causing concern. There was even a notion of digging a moat or canal from Table Bay to False Bay. This would act as a barrier between the indigenous tribes and the settlers. The projected separation of people was based rather on religion than anything else. Christians would live within the area on the western side of the 20 km long moat. Non-believers would live on the eastern side. The possessions of heathens could be seized without sin, and they could be enslaved. Professing Christians, whatever their colour or ethnic origin, could not be kept in bondage or discriminated against in any way. Intermarriage in the slow-growing settlement was common.

The idea of the moat was discarded as being too expensive. Alternative schemes were then considered, including building a line of forts connected by a strong palisade or a thick hedge of wild almond trees running from the banks of the stream known as the Liesbeek, (the name was taken from a kind of water plant) where it flows from the heights of the

Above The hills and well-drained slopes of Constantia have carried vineyards for more than 300 years.

Opposite Rockbound Robben Island has lured many ships to their doom, despite the presence of a lighthouse.

home. How many of them, if any, ever managed to reach their homes is unknown. It would make an epic story.

There was also a feeling that the Cape people sympathised with the slaves and aided their escape. Ill feeling, attacks on farmers, theft of livestock and rumours of war bedevilled the Cape settlers. Even the young girl, Eva, left the settlement with some of her people, wishing Van Riebeeck goodbye with the ominous warning 'Mynheer Van Riebeeck, take good care. I shall not return for a long time, your land will now be full of war.' It was a prophecy that held for centuries.

THE BATTLE FOR THE LAND

When the Cape people returned in 1659 to their traditional grazing grounds, they found them sprinkled with neat farmhouses and tilled fields, all the largesse of the Dutch East India Company showing gratitude to its employees by generous gifts to them of other people's land. The Cape people were enraged.

The Tavern of the Seas was now far too strong to be overrun by force. Doman, the angelic-looking interpreter, had returned to the Cape in 1658 from his visit to Batavia. Abandoning his European clothes, he deserted the fort one night, became an adviser to the Cape people and leader of an aggressive band of cattle thieves. His advice to his followers was to avoid any confrontation with superior European firearms but to harass them at night and in the rain when the old flint firelock guns were almost useless. He had observed that the principal motivation of white people was to make money and he felt that the best way to drive them away was simply to ruin them.

Van Riebeeck organised the freemen and the garrison into a militia and, by indefatigable action, rallied them to strengthen the farmhouses, keep their powder kegs dry, their weapons at the ready and to hold prayer meetings every Wednesday to ask God to withdraw his rage against them. Various reasons were given for this wrath of God, principally the goings-on in the taverns. Van Riebeeck and his superiors had no doubt, however, that the cause of the trouble with the Cape people was the direct result of the occupation of their land. They could no longer even get their livestock to the river to drink without trespassing on private property.

A bounty of 137 shillings and 6 pence was put on the head of Doman, 55 shillings for each of the Cape people taken prisoner, and 27 shillings and 6 pence for each one killed. Vengeance and profit stimulated the militia. Van Riebeeck made plans to build watch houses along the outer line of the settlement.

Early in 1660 the Cape people wished to make their customary journey to the Cape, but they had lost their spirit to fight, and consented to a peace treaty. Another was signed with the upcountry Gorachoukwa. Neither group, however, received much advantage from the agreements:

decrepit to be a worthwhile prize. The Netherlanders relieved the slaver of 250 of the best of the Angolans and then allowed the Portuguese to continue their voyage to Brazil. Of the 250 slaves, 80 died before the *Amersfoort* reached the Cape and the remaining 170 were in a very miserable state. Two weeks later, the *Hasselt* arrived in Table Bay with 228 slaves. Before this influx there were only about twelve individuals in bondage in the Cape and these were from Indonesia and Madagascar.

Eighty-nine of the newcomers were sold off to the local freemen, and the Company put a number into its own bondage. A surplus of 172 was sent on to Batavia. In the Cape the slave owners reconditioned their new acquisitions by feeding them on seal meat, sea birds and eggs from the

islands. The *Hasselt* had brought with the slaves seeds of their staple food, maize, but it would take at least a year before crops could be produced.

A chain of events now began which baffled the slave owners. As soon as the slaves recovered their strength individuals took the first opportunity to run away. They knew vaguely that their homeland was north up the West Coast. They had no idea how far they would have to go or through what dangers of wild animals, hostile people, or the harshness of the desert country they would have to traverse. They simply wanted to go

Above Sun-dappled Government Avenue leads through the Company's Garden.

the Europeans retained possession of the land. The total number of individuals in the pastoral tribes living near the Cape was not more than about 15 000 and of the whole of their race in Southern Africa about 40 000 at most, fragmented and widely scattered. They had to accept the fact of occupation by a stronger power.

Thus ended the first war between African and European people fought in the Cape. Van Riebeeck was delighted. The trade in livestock revived. In the general atmosphere of peace, four successive parties of explorers were sent northwards in search of the Nama people and the city of Davagul or Vigita Magna where the legendary Monomatapa ruled in golden splendour. The Nama people were reached in their arid homeland. Some of them were induced to visit the Cape and peace, friendship and trade were established. Davagul, Vigita Magna and the Monomatapa remained in legends.

THE CHANGING OF THE GUARD

As for Jan van Riebeeck, he had done his best, worked hard and been a loyal servant to his employers. He dreamed of promotion to a position of importance in the East, working with what he called the more orderly people of Asia as a change from the primitive tribes of the Cape. He had been the midwife at the birth of the city of Cape Town but his directors in Holland had little appreciation of this. They often listened to carping accounts by visitors that the Cape was a dreary place, the anchorage exposed to violent gales, the meat tough, the little town a place of lodging and tap houses where strong liquor was sold by persons not having the fear of God before their eyes when they made their charges. In 1660 the directors decided to transfer him to India.

His successor, however, Gerrit Harn, died on the way to the Cape from Holland. It took months before his successor, Zacharias Wagenaar, arrived. In the meantime Van Riebeeck cleared up his effects.

It is interesting to read that when he handed back to the company the farm of Bosheuwel; the improvements included 1 162 young orange, lemon and citron trees, five apple, two pear, nineteen plum, two olive, three walnut, forty-one other fruit trees and several thousand vines. Wagenaar took over the government of the Cape in a ceremony in the fort on 6 May 1662.

Early on the morning of 8 May, Van Riebeeck and his family sailed for Batavia where he was appointed head of the Company's trading station at Malacca. In the three years he remained there as commander, his wife died. He then went to Batavia, married again and was employed by the Company as secretary of the Council of India. He died in 1677.

The fort built by Van Riebeeck has vanished entirely, replaced by the later Castle. It stood on the site of the stalls on the southern side of the Grand Parade. The original vegetable garden, 18 ha in extent, cultivated by Hendrik Boom with the aid of 300 slaves, is now a botanical garden

reduced in size to less than 6 ha. The rest of the former garden is occupied by the buildings of the Houses of Parliament, the town residence of the President of South Africa, the Anglican cathedral of St George the Martyr, the National Library of South Africa, the National Gallery, the South African Museum, the first synagogue in South Africa, built in 1862, and a cluster of buildings housing several departments of the University of Cape Town. An avenue of oak trees 1 km long, known as Government Avenue, traverses the site of the original garden and provides a pleasant walk. Capetonians call it simply 'The Avenue'.

Above Artists and performers hold sway in the traffic-free surrounds of St George's Mall.

In a curious way, the only still living link with Van Riebeeck is a remnant of the almond hedge he planted with the intention of separating the Cape settlement and civilisation, as Van Riebeeck knew it, from primitive Africa. Portions of the hedge still flourish and produce nuts.

There is no known authentic portrait in existence of Van Riebeeck or his wife. The two portraits thought to be of them and often reproduced on postage stamps, bank notes and in books, were proved (in 1984) to be of Bartholomeus Vermuyder and Catharina Kettingh. The two were not even related to each other. They were painted by Dirck Graey and are exhibited in the Amsterdam Rijks Museum. Just how they were palmed off on South Africa as authentic portraits of the Van Riebeecks would make an interesting story.

CHAPTER TWO

GROWING UP

A T THE TIME HE TOOK OVER AT THE CAPE, Zacharias Wagenaar was a conservative servant of the Dutch East India Company, elderly and in poor health. After the volatile Van Riebeeck, the new Commander was not disposed to promote change or development. He was happy to find the Cape peaceful, with deputations from the local tribes visiting the fort to wish him well and cement their friendship by enjoying free jollification. In return, he visited them, dispensing gifts of tobacco and strong drink, and confirming the barter trade for sheep and cattle.

But these were fluid times in Europe; international alliances were constantly changing; indeed the local people never knew whether a visiting ship was friend or foe until it anchored. In this uncertain atmosphere, the Company decided that Van Riebeeck's earth fort was in need of replacement by a more robust stronghold. Plans were drawn up in Holland for a proper stone castle; Wagenaar was empowered to recruit 300 soldiers from passing ships to work on the new fortress while an assortment of convicts and slaves were to be sent to Robben Island to quarry stone and make lime from shells in kilns fired by wood from Houtbaai ('Wood bay'). Commissioner Goske arrived from Holland on 18 August 1665. After eight days of inspections and discussions he selected a site 227 metres southeast of the old fort.

Then began the largest constructional activity so far undertaken in the Cape settlement.

Saturday, 2 January 1666, was a gala day . Practically every resident as well as the crews of visiting ships, soldiers and merchants, all dressed in their best, gathered to see four heavy pieces of stonework lowered into the foundation trench for the massive walls of the projected castle. Tables were spread within the area marked by the foundation trenches, and heavily laden with beef, mutton, vegetables, fruit and eight heavy casks of Cape ale to toast the castle, which had been named Good Hope. There was music and jollification, and the recital of a poem specially composed for the occasion..

Right Time and shade for refreshment in St George's Mall, now free of all vehicular traffic.

THE MIXED SOCIETY

Commander Wagenaar was a sick man at that time. He had already asked the company to relieve him of his post. His successor, Cornelis van Quaelberg, reached the Cape in August 1666 after a dreary voyage lasting eight months, much impeded by weather and the war between Holland and the England of King Charles II. At least the Cape was peaceful when he took over. The pastoral tribes had willy-nilly accepted the reality of their ineffectiveness against the expanding settlement. In any case, their ability to resist had waned. About a fifth of them had died by this time from some unidentified disease. Many of the survivors had moved away to the interior; others took servuce with the settlers or the company and started to merge with the population of slaves of various ethnic origins and especially with the progeny of slave women.

About three-fourths of the children from the slave mothers were from European fathers. White females remained in short supply in the Cape and there was in any case no colour bar. In this mix of humanity the future

ethnic group of the so-called Cape Coloureds had their origin. The slave owners and their conservative allies considered that a directive, issued by the Company and the Church, that all these children be baptised, brought up in the Christian faith, and, as Christians, be free persons even if their fathers disowned them, to be scandalous. The slave mothers, if they became Christian, would also be released from bondage. This threat to the vested interests in slave ownership created a deep schism in the established Dutch Reformed Church. There were unpleasant scenes of protest when slave women brought their half-breed children to be baptised. Cant and great argument split even families into contentious divisions, but Cape slavery endured for almost two centuries.

From its beginning in the first Church in the infant Cape Town, this squabble persisted through the whole story of Southern Africa.

Eva, the young lady interpreter, was the first of the Cape people to become a Christian. Known also as Krotoa, she was baptised early in the regime of Commander Wagenaar. A short while later, on 2 June 1664, she married Pieter van Meerhof, the Danish mercenary soldier and amateur surgeon. There was a bridal feast in the residence of the commander and a wedding gift from the Company of £10. This was the first marriage in the Cape between a couple of African and European origin. Van Meerhof was promoted to the rank of surgeon and overseer of Robben Island. Here the couple made their home and it was here that Eva presented her husband with their first child.

WAR AND PEACE

Work on the new castle proceeded slowly, and then halted – the threat of attack by the English had so diminished following the destruction of their shipping by Admiral De Ruyter in the Thames, that the expense of building a castle at the Cape was no longer a priority. Quarrying on Robben Island was also suspended. Van Meerhof was appointed head of an expedition to Madagascar, where he and eight of his men were killed

Opposite Greenmarket Square was once the city's produce market, and is now a fascinating tangle of craft stalls.

in a clash with the Malagasy at Antongil Bay. Eva, left a widow on Robben Island, went to pieces, became an alcoholic, alternating between loose living on the mainland and disciplinary removals to the Island. She eventually died (in July 1674) and was buried within the church of the castle. A sad ending for an interesting person.

Commander Van Quaelberg also came to grief in the Cape. On 18 June 1668 he was summarily dismissed from his position and relieved by Jacob Borghorst, an invalid who had no desire to remain in the colony. His successor, Peter Hackius, was another sick man – his health had been ruined by long service to the Company in the East. At this stage in his life he was not much inclined to launch new ventures or to do much except keep out of trouble.

The growing town was simply left to its own devices, its buildings increasingly taking on the so-called 'Cape-Dutch' appearance created by the number of Muslims banished from the East and employed as convict or slave builders, aided by the African slaves. They gave subtle variation to the architectural ideas of their European masters.

There was peace with England. The French, however, continued to cause some anxiety by sending fleets around the Cape, anchoring in Table Bay, requesting water and provisions and going into Saldanha Bay to reclaim the old islands of their seal hunters.

In this setting Commander Pieter Hackius died on 30 November 1671 and was buried beneath the floor of the rough building used as a church within the area of the unfinished castle. Until a successor arrived, the Cape was governed by a committee of senior officials, who were instructed to complete the castle to its original design as quickly as possible in order to confront what the Netherlands now considered the inevitability of a war with England and France. These two states had combined in order to seize the rich trade with the East.

THE LEGAL THEFT OF THE CAPE

Since its founding ten years previously, 370 of the Company's ships, 26 French, 9 English and 2 Danish ships were recorded as having visited Cape Town for supplies, having on board over 7 000 crew and passengers. All had drunk of the sweet waters of Table Mountain and replenished their stores from the produce of Van Riebeeck's Tavern of the Seas. The Company now regarded their Cape settlement, not as an infant but as an adolescent in its growth, and upgraded its administration. Even before news of the death of Commander Hackius reached the Netherlands, his

Left The minaret of Mosque Shafee looks over Bo-Kaap. It is one of five mosques in the area.
Opposite Cape mistrels and their colourful costumes are an old tradition, with origins that go back to the days of slavery.

successor had been appointed – Isbrand Goske, the man who had originally selected the site of the castle. He was to have the rank of Governor with a monthly salary of £25, a generous table allowance, formal quarters in the castle as soon as it was ready, and a pleasure house in a garden setting at Rondebosch, where he could relax and entertain visitors. It would be named Rustenburg ('Place of rest'). Two senior officials were appointed at the same time to the posts of Secunde, or second in command and law enforcement officer.

Before the new Governor arrived to take office a ship came in from Batavia bearing one Arnout van Overbeke, a justice of the high court at Batavia and admiral of the return fleet of 1672, who had been commissioned, while the fleet was in Cape Town, to investigate local affairs. His immediate concern was to devise some legal basis for the creation, by the Dutch East India Company, of a colony in the Cape. The area had never been conquered. The settlement had grown unofficially, without the native inhabitants being able to do anything about it. The earliest known hunter-gatherer occupants of the area had been driven out by the pastoral people before Van Riebeeck's arrival. Both these groups were too weak to resist any invader and had no permanent vested interest in the Cape save hunting or grazing.

Since Van Riebeeck's time, Gogoswa, the chief of the principal clan of Cape people, had died. His son Osingkima, known to the Dutch as Prince Schacher, had succeeded him but the local pastoralists had largely disintegrated into small clans. Nevertheless, for want of a more paramount power, Commissioner Van Overbeke offered Prince Schacher £800 worth of assorted goods for the whole of the area from the Peninsula to Saldanha Bay. The pastoralists could graze their animals only where the Company or the freemen did not require the area. Peace was to prevail between the pastoralists and the settlers. The Company would protect Prince Schacher's followers if they were attacked.

Prince Schacher accepted the offer without demur. There was nothing else he could do. His people had already lost the Cape Peninsula to the Company; other parts, such as the area of Saldanha Bay, were the grazing grounds of different groups, but they were not considered. Trade goods of the value of just £2 16s 5d were actually handed over to Prince Schacher to consummate the 'sale'. A similar agreement was signed with the Chainoukwa for the Hottentots Holland area and the False Bay coast. Again the terms were £800 worth of goods for everything, but only £6 16s 4d changed hands, plus assorted junk, liquor and tobacco. The legal gobbledegook of the two agreements, and the cynical complacency of the report to the directors in the Netherlands about the value of the goods actually given to the two pastoral tribes, emphasise the reality of the old proverb, 'a man is not a slave of his word', the basis of so many similar documents drawn up in pretentious legal language.

THE FRONTIER FORTRESS

Governor Goske arrived from Holland on 2 October 1672. News had already reached the Cape that war had commenced between the Netherlands and the combined forces of England, France and two powerful ecclesiastical princes, the elector of Cologne and the Bishop of Munster. It was a formidable force for a small country such as the Netherlands to confront. Moreover, the Dutch were divided by feuds. They were, however, a hardy people and stubborn by nature. The castle being built at the Cape was now considered by the Dutch to be the frontier fortress of India. While they held it they could defy any attempt by their enemies to challenge their dominance in the East.

Governor Goske exerted every effort to complete the castle, meanwhile repairing the earth walls of the old fort. An outpost was also established in the newly acquired Hottentots Holland to which the people of Cape Town could retreat in the event of a successful onslaught on the town by the enemy. There were, at that time, about 600 Europeans resident or stationed in the Cape and times were exciting. An expedition was even organised to capture the British-held island of St Helena. Four ships then in Table Bay were fitted out and their crews augmented with men from the Cape garrison. On 10 January 1673 this pugnacious little force captured St Helena, driving the small British garrison away. Four months later, the British recaptured the island but at least they were aware that an attack on the Cape would require a more considerable force than they had available in the area.

The castle at this time was sufficiently advanced in its construction to allow the garrison to move into it but,. curiously, the urgency diminished – word arrived that the English had made peace with the Dutch. The French at that time lacked the naval power to be regarded as a threat.

Governor Goske had been sent to the Cape expressly to guide it through the troubled times of war, and his task was completed. His successor, Johan Bax, promoted from his post as second officer on the island then known as Ceylon (Sri Lanka), relieved him on 14 March 1676. The new Governor inherited an exuberant little town, full of hope for the future and with only one problem, a 'war' which had been raging in desultory fashion for the previous four years between the neighbouring pastoral tribes. In due course a treaty ended hostilities. The various pastoral chiefs found Governor Bax to be a likable and friendly man.

The castle by then needed only a moat and some finishing touches. As the Company was no longer interested in financing work on the structure, the Governor promulgated a regulation that required everyone, of any rank or sex, to contribute labour towards the digging of the moat. To set an example, Bax, his wife and little son, all the Company's officers and the leading inhabitants of the town, gathered together and spent some time in excavation. Over the next months work steadily extended the moat but

unhappily the Governor, although young and healthy, did not live to see its completion. He caught a cold during the hard winter and died on 29 June 1678, leaving the second in command to control affairs until the Company appointed a successor.

GOVERNOR SUPREME

The new man only reached the Cape from the Netherlands on 12 October 1679. He was rated only as a Commander, for peace made the Cape less important, but he was to prove one of the most energetic men ever to be head of affairs anywhere in Southern Africa. His name was Simon van der Stel. He was the eldest son of Adriaen van der Stel of Dordrecht, Commander of the Dutch East India Company troops then engaged in the conquest of Ceylon (Sri Lanka). Shortly after his arrival in Ceylon, Adriaen was captured in battle, decapitated, and his head displayed on a spear to the Dutch troops and his family. Simon's mother was Maria Lievens, born in Batavia from a slave mother. .

The Dutch East India Company had an obligation to the families of their employees. In 1659, Simon van der Stel was sent to the Netherlands to complete his education. When he finished his schooling he was employed by the Company and on 23 October 1663 married Johanna Jacoba Six, daughter of a well-to-do Amsterdam family. Over the next thirteen years he showed great competence in his work and was then rewarded with the offer of the post as Commander of the Cape. It was a big career opportunity at a far superior salary and he accepted with enthusiasm. His wife declined to accompany her husband to the Cape. Her health was poor and she remained in the comfort of Amsterdam until her death in 1700. Van der Stel's four sons, Willem, Adriaan, Hendrik and Frans, and his daughter Catharina, together with his wife's younger sister Cornelia, sailed with him, so he was well supported on the voyage.

When they landed on 12 October 1679 they were received with such pomp as the Cape could mount to honour a new Commander – discharges of cannon and musketry, the cheers of onlookers who saw their new head of government as a short, dark-complexioned man, refined of manner, courteous, highly intelligent and very alert. For the next twenty years Simon van der Stel was to control the colony. He was destined never to leave the Cape that he loved.

Shortly after his arrival Van der Stel rode out to examine the countryside, encamping on the banks of a small tributary to the Eerste ('First') River, the principal watercourse draining one of the loveliest and most fertile parts of Africa, a domain of wild flowers destined to rank among the principal wine and fruit farming lands of the Western Cape. It was then

Opposite Trails of black mussel shells mark the tidal flow at Blouberg beach, where a British army stormed ashore in 1806.

empty of people, free of any pollution and serenely beautiful. For five days Van der Stel explored this wild garden of infinite charm, following the Eerste River towards its source in the bosom of the mountains, a place which captivated him completely. Here there was no sign of other human beings. In his mind he saw a picture of a thriving agricultural community, of rich crops and fat cattle grazing on the green pastures, drinking their fill of the amber coloured water of the streams. He returned to the castle and began to fulfil his dreams of a new Holland on the southern part of the vast continent of Africa.

Before the year ended the first settler had occupied ground at Stellenbosch. Next year eight families followed this; all had been tempted by the offer of as much free land as they could cultivate, selected by themselves, and only to be reclaimed by the Company if they ceased to cultivate it. The sole obligation to the Company was a tithe of the grain grown by the farmers. There was free grazing on all uncultivated land.

Cape Town also received Van der Stel's beneficial attention. The Company garden was replanned, divided into separate plots, some devoted to vegetables, others to fruit, still others experimental plantations of timber trees collected from all over the world. The wild flowers, herbs and trees of the Cape were also planted and studied to discover their special uses. Van der Stel enlarged the garden on its southern side and, on the north, eventually built a large hospital and a lodge in which the Company slaves were housed. A pleasure lodge made its appearance on the site of the present statue of Queen Victoria. Pathways and an avenue were laid out. Many visitors told Van der Stel that nowhere else in the world was there a more varied display of trees and plants in so beautiful a setting.

Wide, straight streets were laid out, while trees in great number were planted to provide shade, rest the eye, and beautify a town where the buildings were mainly a dazzling white from the use of the limewash which protected walls.

THE MAGIC CIRCLE

Increasingly, the buildings carried in their design a touch of the East as well as of Africa and Europe. Prisoners and political exiles from Indonesia and India, many of them cultured and highly intelligent men, were being sent to the Cape. These personages, generally accompanied by a handful of followers and family members, at first felt themselves dreadfully detached from their familiar Eastern society. But they received a little comfort when one of them, a man of great influence, Khardi Abdusalem, urged them to hold their faith without fear for they would one day live protected by a holy circle of kramats (saintly places) which would come into being at the tombs of holy men who would constantly intercede on their behalf with Allah. A line drawn connecting these kramats would form a magic ring. Within it the residents of Cape Town, not only Muslims, would live safe

from fire, famine, plague, earthquake, tidal wave or attack by hostile forces. Among high-born exiles from Java was the revered Sheik Yussuf of Macassar, a man of powerful influence and a thorn in the flesh to the Dutch colonists in the East. He died, on the then isolated farm Zandvliet, in May 1677. His burial place was the first and most important of the kramats in the magic circle around Cape Town.

Sheik Yussuf's tomb is now an impressive memorial, built in 1925 by Hadji Sullaiman Shah. The kramat is on a low hill with a grand view of mountains and farmlands. It is close to the banks of the Eerste River, for the sound of running water is not only pleasant but is said to have magical curative powers. Five other kramats complete the magic circle around Cape Town. Close to the road followed by countless people to the viewsite on the summit of Signal Hill, there is a pretty little domed building, resting place of Sayed Muhammad Hassan Gaibi Shah. On the slopes of Signal Hill, above the old quarry at the top of Strand Street, is the third Kramat, where lie the bodies of four holy men: Khardi Abdusalem, Tuan Syed, Tuan Guru and Tuan Nurman.

The magic circle then leads to Oudekraal where, from the scenic drive of Victoria Road, a concrete stairway rises beneath the trees to a kramat where lies buried Nureel Mobeen, who is said to have been banished to Robben Island. He escaped by swimming to the mainland supported on a plank. For the rest of his life he hid in the bush of Oudekraal. In his time he is said to have performed many miracles.

The fifth kramat in the magic circle is on Robben Island – the tomb of Sayed Abdurahman Matura, Prince of Ternate, an island in the Molucca sea of Indonesia. He was banished to Robben Island in January 1744 and died there in 1755. The sixth kramat is on the slopes of Islam Hill in the Constantia valley, close to the stream known as the Spaanschemat. Nearby, at the entrance gate to the farm Klein Constantia, again beside a running stream, there is the tomb of Abdumaah Shah.

The paths to these places are well trodden, and have not been forgotten. To 'make the circle', to visit each one of the kramats, is much desired by all devout Cape Muslims.

SLAVERY, CRIME AND PUNISHMENT

In October 1684, the Company's governing body, the Assembly of Seventeen, appointed one of its members, Hendrik Adriaan van Rheede, the Lord of Mydrecht, to head a commission to examine the affairs of the Cape and those of Ceylon and Hindustan. According to the colonial norms of the time the Cape was doing well. It was not only feeding itself and profiting handsomely from supplying ships but even starting to export food to the East. As far as its social system went, it was amazing how readily people from Europe adjusted their thinking to a slave-based colonial society. In their home countries slavery might be repugnant but by simply

crossing an ocean they could walk ashore into a new world of buying, selling and ruthless exploitation of human beings. Such a society, in fact, perfectly revealed man's inhumanity to man with not the slightest awareness of any wrong to it.

The Lord of Mydrecht found nothing too objectionable in slavery in the Cape, though he tried to improve things with a law that offered freedom to imported slaves (of both sexes) after 30 years of bondage, and to slaves born in the Cape on reaching the age of 40. In contradiction, though, these men and women could be freed only as a favour on the part of the owner. As a rule owners were reluctant to free slaves until they were so old as to be useless. In order to save feeding them they were then emancipated, and driven out to fend for themselves, usually by begging or as vagrants living in destitution in caves or crude shelters on the mountain slopes, where they were known as 'Bergies'. His lordship also made it a law that slave children under the age of twelve were to be sent to school, where they were to be taught the principles of Christianity, to read, write and conduct themselves respectfully to their superiors.

Some restrictions, too, were placed on punishment. Excessive retribution drove slaves to desert and turn criminal. Fugitives who were captured were to be flogged and chained as a warning to others, but such punishment could only be inflicted with the consent of the authorities. Punishment generally, to law breakers of any colour, remained severe. Robben Island was always accommodating. The slight rise at Green Point called Gallows Hill possessed a gibbet capable of hanging seven or more condemned persons at a time. Around it were the grim means for torture and execution by impalement or breaking at the wheel, sometimes from the feet up in order to prolong agony. There were ten wheels used for this limb-breaking.

So far as relations with the indigenous population were concerned, the original inhabitants had either dispersed or fragmented to insignificant numbers. The local Sonkwa (or Bushmen) were nearly extinct. The pastoral tribes living further from the Cape, such as the Hessekwa, the Inkwa and the Outenikwa along the coast to the east, were friendly and prepared to trade significant amounts of their livestock for the usual junk.

From the west coast, the Namakwa sent several representatives to meet the Commissioner. They came riding into town seated on trained oxen. Some of these oxen also carried on their backs the simple skin huts which these nomads were accustomed to take with them as they wandered with their herds and flocks in search of pasture. Even more interesting were the fine samples of copper ore which they showed the Dutch authorities. Where there was copper there might be gold.

Opposite The kramat or burial place of a Muslim holy man on Signal Hill is one of several such places.

The Lord of Mydrecht was pleased that Van der Stel had already sent three expeditions (unfortunatéy abortive) up the west coast to reach what were called the copper mountains. Prospectors were also busy fossicking through the mountains of the Cape Peninsula hoping to find such precious metals as gold and silver. One prospect shaft in the Steenberge (present-day Silvermine) had already yielded a strange ore which the people of Cape Town excitedly thought was silver. This was eventually identified in Holland as manganese but the discovery at least stimulated what was the beginning of systematic prospecting in Southern Africa. Van der Stel was authorised to personally lead an expedition to the copper mountains of the Nama people.

COLONIAL PROGRESS

The Lord of Mydrecht also approved of the foundation of Stellenbosch and the generous grants of free land there to stimulate settlement. In Holland every effort was already being made by the Company to attract immigrants to the Cape, with particular attention to females. Van der Stel himself was rewarded with a superbly situated piece of ground beyond the last farm then occupied at Wynberg. He named it Constantia, presumably in honour of the young daughter of Commissioner Rijkloff van Goens, who had that name, or simply because the name meant 'constancy'.

Van der Stel now launched himself into a considerable programme of work. In August 1685 he set out, with about 100 men, on an exploratory journey northwards to Nama country, which everyone hoped was a venture leading to the discovery of vast wealth, not only of copper, but of many precious metals and gemstones. The explorers, after many adventures, reached the Copper Mountains on 21 October and, guided by the Nama people, found copper ore of great richness and quantity. But the two months it had taken to reach the area had seen the explorers forced to penetrate such rugged, arid country that there could be no way of carrying heavy ore all the way to Cape Town on the transport of the day. The dream of a huge and instant profit for the Company, which had obsessed every commander of the Cape since Van Riebeeck, still proved elusive. The richness of the samples of copper ore tantalised everybody who saw them but it was to be 200 years before the copper mines of Namaqualand were to come into production.

Van der Stel was always a great man for trees. The Cape was not well wooded, except in the mountain gorges, where the forests were fragile and already over-exploited for fuel and timber. Experimental work in the

Left The manor house and vineyards of Buitenverwachting nestle below Constantiaberg.
Opposite Buitenverwachting wears the classic symmetry of the Cape Dutch style of architecture.

Company's garden indicated that imported oaks would do best in local conditions. Van der Stel launched an extensive programme of cultivation, and by the spring of 1687 there were over 50 000 oaks in the nurseries and 5 000 planted out.

Stellenbosch, in the short time of its existence, was already showing signs of its future destiny as the prettiest town in Southern Africa. An annual fair was inaugurated in the town in 1686. Each year, from the 1st to the 14th of October, became a holiday season for the people of the Cape. They travelled to Stellenbosch to buy and sell without any restriction, to feast and drink the products of the country, to play games and compete in gun shooting at a target traditionally shaped like a parrot. A church, courthouse, residence for the magistrate and a mill all made their appearance in 1686.

Van der Stel also undertook experimentation in agriculture. Crops such as rice, cassava, hops and olives were all tried without success. Vines were doing well but the wine was poor. The quality from the Stellenbosch farms was better than from anywhere else in the Cape but not up to the wines of Europe. Van der Stel planted vines obtained from many countries, even from Iran (Persia), the reputed home of the grape.

Immigrants arrived, and were settled in the Drakenstein valley – 23 families in 1687 and, in the following year, the first batch of a stream of French Protestant Huguenot refugees who had fled religious persecution in France. Van der Stel was delighted, although he would have preferred them to be Dutch. The Huguenots were, however, fine farming stock, a few of them were experienced viticulturists and, importantly, most of them were married. They established themselves on glorious farmlands in what became known as Franschhoek ('French glen'), at the upper valley of the Berg River.

CAPE TOWN'S PROBLEMS
The Cape prospered, notwithstanding the shortage of marriageable females, which continued to be a source of social problems. Each year saw more shipping anchoring in Table Bay, and in the bay close to Cape Point around which Simon's Town would develop. The growth of the colony generally, and the esteem in which Simon van der Stel was held by his directors in Holland, was marked on 1 June 1691 when the Commander was elevated to the dignity of a Governor.

But Cape Town had its problems. Garbage collection was left to the hyenas and other scavengers which came down each night from lairs on the mountain slopes and wandered at will through the dark streets. Heavy drinking and gambling in the taverns led to fights and murders. There was no police force. The shortage of females was the cause of violent brawls. Even slave women were in short supply, and their men's immorality was a source of concern to the authorities..

Lions and leopards still frequented the countryside, occasionally venturing into the little town and dragging away the odd drunkard who had fallen asleep on the roadside. Gangs of runaway slaves provided a hard-core criminal element. These last were a community of the lost. Their destitution and hopeless future gave them no alternative but to resort to robbery while the brutality of punishment when they were caught made them desperate. To die on the gallows was at least a quick way out but sentences of torture 'close to death', impalement, or to be broken on the rack or wheel was the more usual punishment, with the mangled wretch dumped to die on Gallows Hill. The only possible mercy came from one of their comrades creeping into the town at night to put them out of their misery by strangulation.

Pollution of drinking water was becoming a health hazard. Even the once pure Fresh River on which the shipping depended was carrying down to the sea unpalatable run off from dirty streets and the dirtier habits of human beings using it for washing their persons, clothes, utensils and as a form of waterborne sewage disposal. The southeast wind of summer, known as the Cape Doctor, fortunately blew most of the stinks, miasmas and assorted bugs, insects and bacteria away and kept the town healthier than its population deserved.

An endless stream of thirsty and amorous sailors called at the Cape. Most of them were the crews and passengers of the Dutch East Indiamen. Amongst this motley company the majority were reasonably honest merchants, but others were pirates. Slave traders also frequented Table Bay, mainly taking human cargoes from East Africa, Mozambique and Madagascar to the West Indies, but always prepared to oblige local demand for what were advertised as sturdy, stout Negroes, male or female. Auctions of slaves were periodically held on what became known as Church Square, a piece of waste land, once a marsh, which adjoined the grounds of the present Groote Kerk with its pleasant, leisurely sounding two-note clock chime marking the passing of the hours. A small monument in Bureau Street marks the site.

Governor Van der Stel did nothing to ease the degradation of slavery. The dual morality of the time made the lot of those in bondage of little concern to the rest of the community. The development of the Governor's own estate of Constantia was based on slave labour and there was no available substitute. At least, however, he made Cape Town, for all of its people, a far more agreeable place in which to live. The Heerengracht was improved; a new road was constructed along the line of the canal known as the Keisersgracht (which took water from the Fresh River to the castle moat) and much later named after C.H. Darling, the British Lieutenant-Governor of the Cape from 1852 to 1854. On the seaward side of this road, work began in 1697 on levelling the ground and this became the Grand Parade.

Most important of all was the building of the new hospital, larger, far better and more suitably located on a site between the upper end of the Heerengracht and Berg Street (now St George's Street). This was the last work by Van der Stel in his capacity as Governor. In 1696 he requested permission to resign his office and retire to his estate of Constantia. The directors gave him a final honour when they appointed his eldest son, Willem Adriaan, born in 1664, as his successor.

THE PASSING OF A GOVERNOR
On 11 February Van der Stel left the castle and removed to his estate, Constantia. For the next thirteen years he lived there, farming, ranching cattle, planting thousands of oak trees and vines and producing fine wine. His reputation for hospitality, good food and wine attracted innumerable visitors to what was regarded as one of the most beautiful properties in the world. He obtained more grants of land, and grazing rights for his cattle until he controlled practically the entire Cape Peninsula outside the settled area of Cape Town. He ran a fishing and sealing industry at Saldanha Bay and was altogether a man for all seasons and activities. His one great disappointment came from his son, whose governance foundered in accusations of oppression and venality. Willem was recalled to Holland on 3 June 1707.

Simon van der Stel was left in the Cape without the companionship of any of his family. As death approached he became despondent. In his last will and testament, his scribe wrote: 'His excellency was overcome with the evil and weakness of human life, passing away like a shadow, knowing that nothing is more certain than death and, in contrast, nothing more uncertain than man's time and span upon this earth.'

He bequeathed Constantia to his five children. None of them was interested in the estate, other than as a source of financial inheritance. Simon van der Stel died at Constantia on 24 June 1712.

After the estate was wound up it was divided into three sections in order to make it more saleable. Over the decades there was a succession of owners; the property went into decline until it was sold, in 1778, to Hendrik Cloete of Stellenbosch. A glorious revival then took place.

There is no known completely authentic portrait of Van der Stel. A canvas showing a man thought to have been him, in a hunting party and considered nine-tenths authentic, was unfortunately destroyed in 1963 in a fire in the Napier collection in Ireland. Only a photograph of this painting remains. A second portrait, also of a huntsman, but of less authenticity, is in the The Hague's Rijksdienst Beeldende Kunst. This portrait, however, is only considered one-tenth possible and nine-tenths of dubious authenticity.

Opposite On Wednesday and Saturday mornings the Grand Parade is a bustling marketplace.

CHAPTER THREE

CITY, BAY AND ISLAND

As cities go, Cape Town, compared with those ancient places of Asia and Europe, is still a mere juvenile. In its relatively brief three and a half centuries, however, it has experienced interesting, sometimes dramatic times and gathered memories of odd events and diverse people who have come to the Tavern of the Seas, dallied for perhaps just a little while or, beguiled by its beauty and atmosphere, remained for the rest of their lives.

Many of those who landed on the shores of Table Bay did so involuntarily. They were wrecked there. During the winter months when the prevailing wind was the northwester, the bay could become a death trap for shipping. There was simply no shelter from this wind, which can blow gale force for a merciless hour then deceptively lull, while it recovers breath for another big blow. Over 200 ships have come to grief in Table Bay.

A particularly famous wreck occurred during a storm on 1 June 1773. The Dutch East Indiaman *De Jonge Thomas* ran aground and began breaking up in the pounding of heavy surf. Employed as a dairyman by the Dutch East India Company was 65-year-old Wolraad Woltemade, who saw that the crew of the ship were almost helpless against the power of the sea. He rode his horse through the waves seven times, each time returning with two men holding on. On the eighth attempt he and his horse were themselves overwhelmed by a huge wave and drowned.

THE STRUGGLE FOR A HARBOUR

The loss of life, ships and cargo from winter storms was the principal disadvantage of the Cape victualling station. With the means available at that time it was very difficult to do anything about this problem. Engineering on a massive scale was the answer but this would demand a lot of expenditure. After the disastrous storms of May 1737, attempts were made to create a breakwater (or mole) at what became known as Mouille Point on the western side of Table Bay, but although a lot of work was done (farmers bringing wagon-loads of produce for sale in Cape Town were required

Right The view from Robben Island shows the peaks of the Twleve Apostles next to Table Mountain.

to use their empty vehicles to transport one load of stones to the site), nothing came of the venture.

No further progress was made in providing artificial shelter in Table Bay although periodic northwesterly winds continued to create havoc. In 1831 six ships were wrecked and the British government, who then controlled the Cape, were sufficiently disturbed to appoint the first Harbour Board, directed to construct a stone pier from the bottom of Bree Street. This was completed but it proved to be almost useless. A second stone pier was then built from the foot of Adderley Street, together with a wooden pier near the site of the original stone jetty built by Van Riebeeck in 1656. None of these works provided any shelter for ships.

It was only in 1856 that Captain James Vetch, harbour surveyor to the British Admiralty, produced a plan for an enclosed harbour in Table Bay. The plan included an inner and an outer basin, protected by two breakwater piers – a scheme subsequently modified to save money. John Coode was appointed engineer-in-chief. The following year a prodigious

gale stormed into the bay. For three days a northwest wind blew at overwhelming force. Sixteen large ships and seven smaller boats were wrecked. The storm died, the sun shone, but five days later, on 14 June, the storm returned and wrecked two more big ships.

After a disaster of this magnitude construction of a proper harbour had to start, no matter the cost. It had an auspicious beginning. On 17 September 1860, Prince Alfred, the 16-year-old second son of Queen Victoria, at the start of a tour of the Cape Colony and Natal, pulled a silver trigger to tip the first truckload of stones into 1,8 metres of water to start the new breakwater. A bronze plaque on a stone pillar on East Pier road marked this construction which eventually, with the help of convict labour, resulted in the man-made harbour of Table Bay, a major engineering accomplishment by any world standard. The Prince was a fitting man to launch so considerable a work. At the time of his visit to Cape Town he was a midshipman on the steam frigate *Euryalus* with ahead of him a distinguished lifelong career in the Royal Navy. His tour, the first royal tour of South Africa, was undertaken mainly on horseback, from Cape Town along the coast to Durban, then over the Drakensberg to the Orange Free State where he was entertained to the greatest hunt known in history with the shooting on the farm Bainsvlei west of Bloemfontein of several thousand head of antelope in one afternoon of 'sport'. The prince shot 24 of the animals.

Prince Alfred visited Cape Town on three more occasions. In 1867, as captain of the steam frigate *Galatea*, he laid the foundation stone of what was named the Alfred Dock. After the ceremony he travelled to Knysna, where he hunted elephants in the forest in company with the well-known Rex family, the Governor of the Cape Colony, Sir Philip Wodehouse, and a considerable party of staff and dignitaries. He was back in December 1868 and again in 1870, at which time officially opened the completed Alfred Basin and, at the same time, laid the foundation stone for a drydock that was to be named, in 1881, after Sir Hercules Robinson, Governor

Opposite The Tavern of the Seas offers safe and sheltered anchorage to vessels plying the East-West trade route.

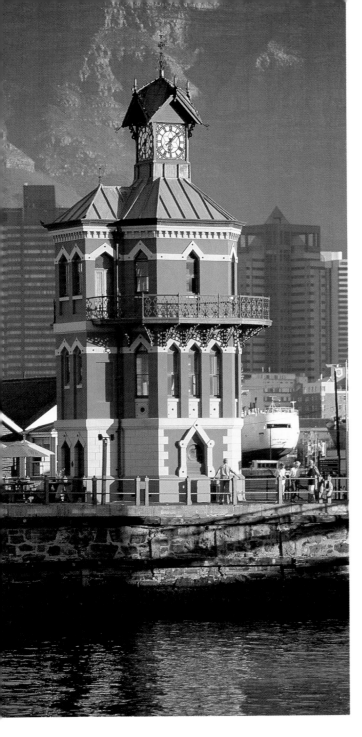

of the Cape. The attractive clock and signalling tower at the entrance to the basin was built in 1883. The entrance is so narrow that it was from the beginning a problem to pilots and shipmates. It was known as the Cut. A small flat-bottomed double-ended ferryboat known as the Penny Ferry provided a service for pedestrians wishing to cross the Cut. The first ferryman, Abdul, spent his lifetime working the boat and was estimated at the time of his retirement to have covered a distance equal to twice around the world.

DREDGING DEEP
In 1890, 1000 labourers and 600 convicts, housed in what was called the Breakwater Prison, commenced work on extending the breakwater to 1 430 metres in order to protect a water area of 27 hectares, creating what was named the Victoria Basin, with jetties and a new south pier. It took five years of work to complete this phase of development. Larger ships could then call at Table Bay and be berthed in safety, but the outbreak of the Anglo-Boer war and a massive increase in shipping made the whole new facility inadequate within four years.

The end of the war in 1902 provided some relief from the pressure on the harbour but by 1925 the situation was impossible with ever-larger ships demanding deeper water and bigger berths. Work on a new basin on the southeastern side of the Victoria Basin began in 1926. There was, however, a limit to the size of the new basin. In 1913 the Cape Town municipality had constructed a recreation pier projecting from the foot of Adderley Street. For the time being, new harbour works were confined to the northwest side of this pier. The new basin was opened in 1932. It was 75 hectares in extent. It had a wide entrance to allow larger ships to berth in sheltered conditions, but a serious problem was soon revealed.

On 25 January 1936, the biggest ship so far to visit South African waters, the 43 000 ton *Empress of Britain*, arrived at dawn in Table Bay after a record-breaking run from Madeira. The liner was carrying 387 wealthy passengers, including 30 millionaires, on a cruise around the world and their arrival was considered to be of major publicity value in the development of a South African tourism industry.

The ship was docked at B berth without difficulty. Entertainment and tours around the Cape Peninsula and inland had been arranged for the passengers until the planned sailing time at noon on 28 January. A vicious southeaster, however, blew up and gleefully showed its power. The big ship was pressed so firmly against the quay that all the port's tugboats and all the port's men could not get the *Empress of Britain* out to sea again. At least, not until the southeaster died down. It took its own time.

The great liner left 30 hours late and this was a sad embarrassment to the Table Bay harbour. The battle between man and ship against the wind had been well reported around the world. A big audience of spectators watched every effort by the tugboats. At 6.37 pm on 29 January there was a little lull. The tugboats were waiting for the chance. They managed to get the ship out just in time. By 8 pm the wind was back at over 100 km an hour but the liner was far gone by then, heading around the Cape of Good Hope at full speed for Durban and India.

A new harbour scheme was launched involving major engineering construction and dredging work. Time was of the essence: World War II loomed; the navies of the free world would need a bigger and better port of call at the southern tip of Africa. The municipal pier had to be demolished together with most of the abortive new basin construction. Two new quay walls parallel to each other, 1 000 metres long and 670 metres apart, had to be built extending from the Woodstock beach towards the Victoria Basin; massive dredging of the area between the two walls yielded a spoil which had to be pumped by pipeline and deposited on the land (south) side of the project, completely burying the original shore and the historic landing place of Roggebaai. The spoil provided 140 hectares of landfill, known as the Foreshore, as a brand-new and very welcome addition to the available building space of the city area of Cape Town, already feeling somewhat compressed between sea and mountains.

It was a spectacular engineering concept. The dredging operation started on 15 May 1935. By the outbreak of the war on 3 September 1939, 117 hectares of what was named the Duncan Dock, after Sir Patrick Duncan, Governor-General of the Union of South Africa, was in use. The contract originally intended the whole new harbour to be completed by 8 July 1941 but the war delayed completion until 1 July 1945. The new harbour included a small craft harbour presided over by the Royal Cape Yacht Club, and the largest graving dock – it was named the Sturrock Dock – in the southern hemisphere, 360 metres long, 47,6 metres wide and 13,7 metres deep. Bulk storage space for coal and liquid fuel was provided, as well as a 27 220 ton grain elevator and pre-cooling stores for 29 000 tons of fruit for what is the third-largest fruit export harbour in the world. There is also a floating dock capable of lifting 1 016 tons.

In 1966, a new bulk tanker berth on the northeastern (seaward) mole of the Duncan Dock was opened. It is connected by three pipelines to the oil refinery at Milnerton. The containerisation of maritime cargoes has resulted in further development, both in the harbour and inland at Paarden Eiland. Progress has also meant the complete disappearance of Woodstock Beach, once a cherished Cape Town amenity.

Left The elegant Clock Tower was once the Port Captain's office, from which he could overlook the entire harbour.

Opposite The Waterfront is once of Cape Town's most visited venues, and first in a survey of tourist destinations.

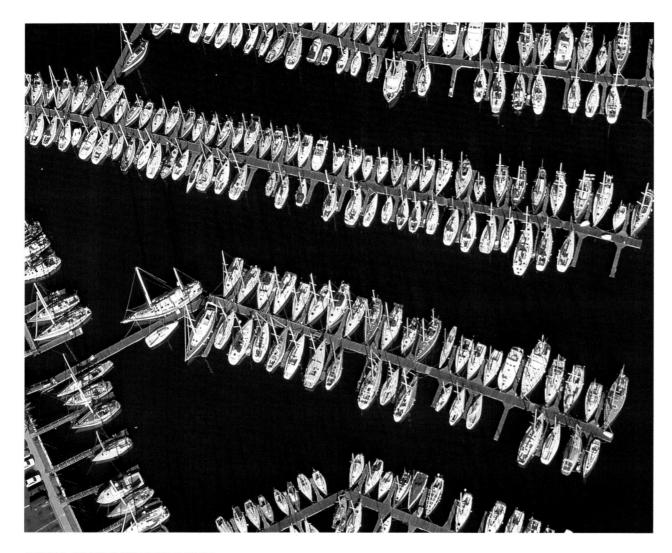

BIRTH OF THE WATERFRONT

Table Bay is the principal passenger and mail harbour of Southern Africa, and a haven for repairing, revictualling and refuelling passing ships. Its fishing industry is enormous, as nine-tenths of the fish eaten in South Africa is landed, processed and railed from Cape Town. From the harbour, South African trawlers work the Agulhas Bank; while fishing fleets from many foreign countries, far outnumbering the local ships, use Table Bay as a base, trans-shipping their catches onto refrigerated vessels for transport to their home countries, replenishing their own stores and fuel, and allowing their crews spells of shore leave.

In 1969, the contracts were awarded for a new outer basin especially for the use of container ships. Heavy blasting of the rock of the seabed was needed to provide this new harbour with 22 deep-water berths. It was completed in 1975 and named after Ben Schoeman, the then Minister of Transport who opened it on 1 July 1977. The spoil from the dredging of

Above The Royal Cape Yacht Club has its home in a well-occupied corner of the Duncan Dock.

this massive work provided the material for a new foreshore area of 180 hectares which buried the original coastline of Table Bay on the southeast side of the new harbour. This area is known as Paarden Eiland, which means island of horses: back in the 1780s Arend van Kielligh, contractor of wagons and horses to the Dutch East India Company, grazed his livestock here. It was loosely defined as the area between the mouths of the Salt River and the Diep River, which flows south from Rietvlei and forms the Milnerton lagoon. Sailors from the stranded *Haarlem* set up their camp in this vicinity in 1647 and demonstrated the potential of Table Bay as a European settlement. It remains at least something of an island, completely overgrown not with lush vegetation but with a hodgepodge of factories.

After all these large-scale harbour works, the historic Alfred Basin, still in use mainly by fishing vessels, with the waterfront facing into the Victoria Basin, was starting to look somewhat woebegone, its warehouses and other structures, architecturally interesting but showing their Victorian age. Their neglect put them in peril of demolition and there was some controversy as to what would replace them if they were sold off to the tender mercies of property speculators. In the end it was decided that the Victoria and Alfred working harbours be maintained as a colourful, animated, lively centrepiece for the revitalisation of the waterfront buildings for tourism, entertainment and related uses. The concept was largely the vision of Mike Myburgh, the Assistant General Manager of SA Harbours. It was brilliant.

In November 1988, Transnet established its first private company, Victoria & Alfred Waterfront (Pty) Ltd. Brian Kantor, head of the School of Commerce of the University of Cape Town, was appointed chairman with David Jack as managing director. In the first five years of the ongoing project, the fading waterfront was transformed like a Cinderella. Prince Alfred and his revered mother would have been more than delighted to have their names attached to such a glittering princess. Restaurants, cafés, cinemas, theatres, hotels, a waterfront brewery, innumerable speciality shops, the headquarters of the National Sea Rescue Institute, a mineral world with wonderful displays of gemstones and a scratch patch with finders keepers for all manner of lovely things, arts and crafts, a vast sea world aquarium, boat trips, the SA Maritime Museum, a giant Imax cinema, the endless movement of shipping, the old Breakwater Prison converted into the University of Cape Town's Graduate School of Business, seals basking on ledges as a lazy contrast to the coming, going, promenading, meandering and search by human beings for fun and food, day and night, in what has become one of the major tourism and recreational attractions of Southern Africa. The story of the man-made harbour of Table Bay has gone far from the very first attempt to provide a sanctuary for shipping.

Opposite Still waters belie the bustle within the graceful buildings of the Waterfront.

THE ISLAND

The ferry for Robben Island has its base in the Victoria Basin. It is fitting at this stage in the story of the Tavern of the Seas to take the 13 km journey across Table Bay to Murray's Bay, the island's neat, modern little harbour.

In 1806 the new British administration at the Cape was just starting to appreciate the varied charms and values of Robben Island. Its convenience

Above Bontebok, once an endangered species, are among the contented exiles of Robben Island.

as an isolation centre was obvious. In 1807 a superintendent was appointed and unwanted persons were thenceforth ferried over to be placed under his charge. These persons included young army officers who had got themselves into debt or some personal trouble, and were sent to the island to hunt rabbits and be kept out of mischief. But most of the other arrivals were human wrecks of various sorts. Very little money was provided to maintain this growing population of outcasts. Government authority had the happy notion that such people could simply be swept away, dumped with little prospect of ever returning, or of seeing their

friends and relatives again. They were considered to be the living dead, and only rarely were relatives allowed to visit them.

At that time it was a wretched place. The sick, mad and criminal were herded together in a number of shacks. They had nothing to do save look longingly at the distant Table Mountain and potter about the shore, fishing and gathering shellfish from the rocks and fishing. Then the superintendent hit upon a scheme to set one person to watch another, which provided the outcasts with occupation, and created such dissent and mutual suspicion that there was little prospect of rebellion or escape.

Persons banished to the island for political reasons formed a special group. They were generally individuals of some stature and intelligence. They found conditions on the island particularly intolerable with escape constantly on their minds. Several tried, some succeeded, but the sea was bitterly cold and the currents hazardous. Makhanda, the revered Xhosa mystic who led his followers on an abortive, bloody attack on Grahamstown on 22 April 1819, was one of the political prisoners. On the night of 9 August 1828 he led 30 other prisoners in a resolute attempt to escape. They overpowered their guards, seized the whaling boats on the beach of Murray's Bay and set out for the mainland. Reaching the shore, the excited men, sensing freedom, plunged into the surf and made for the beach. Only Makhanda failed to reach the shore. He was drowned. The rest of the men scattered in several parties. Three of them were captured, others were shot, and some escaped. The three captured men, including one named John Smith, were hanged, their heads then fixed on stakes and mounted on Robben Island as a warning to others.

As for Makhanda, such was his mystic reputation that for over 50 years the Xhosa people refused to accept that he was dead. They called him Nxele and affirmed that one day he would return to lead them to victory against the whites. His personal mats, clothes and ornaments, were carefully kept for him. When, at last, all hope for his return was abandoned, a proverb found a lasting place with the Xhosa people, *Kukuza kuka Nxele* (the coming of Nxele), said to anybody who longed for something which would never happen.

In 1843 a considerable change came to Robben Island when it was proposed that all the common convicts be brought back to the mainland and set to work building roads. The accommodation vacated by the convicts would be available for the housing of lepers, lunatics, beggars, paupers, chronically and terminally ill people, cripples and the blind. Political prisoners would remain on the island. Quite a considerable exchange of island population took place, which prompted new construction. A substantial house was built for the superintendent, quarters for the military personnel who did tours of guard duty, a bakery, butchery, blacksmith's shop and other conveniences. A neat little Anglican church had been built in 1841 by Captain R.J. Wolfe, who later settled at Wynberg. A 200 metre long jetty made its appearance in 1847, and a regular village started to grow as a centre for the island.

Conditions for the sick remained primitive. The lepers, particularly, lived in complete squalor. Their hospital was hopelessly overcrowded, with the kitchen acting after meals as a bathroom. Perhaps understandably, the lepers were described as a parcel of desperate characters, idle, insolent, insubordinate and, knowing the then incurable nature of their disease, reckless to a degree. Without adequate funds the succession of medical superintendents could do little and some of them were not particularly notable for their ability. The island cemetery grew larger year by year.

Conditions improved after 1861 when, following a government inquiry, Dr William Edmunds was appointed as medical superintendent and more money was provided. The island was cleaned up; its 'capital' grew into a pretty village unofficially known as Irishtown because most of the nurses and officials stationed there came from Ireland. With such a community it could only be lively. There were dances and romances, picnics among the arum lilies or next to one of the great rock pools. Edmund's Pool was a favourite with its underwater forests of marine vegetation, anemones of exquisite colour and quaintly patterned little fish so tame that at the first sign of a picnic they rose to the surface in eager anticipation of a share of at least the crumbs of the good things of life. The main street of Irishtown had a tramway with mule-drawn trolleys. Schools were built as well as a library, recreation hall, fire station and general dealer. A second church, constructed from island stone and designed by the celebrated architect Herbert Baker, was built in 1895 by the lepers and named the 'Church of the Good Shepherd'.

On the summit of Vuurberg (now Minto Hill), the highest point of the island and the site of the first navigation beacon on the South African coast, a neat, permanent lighthouse was erected in 1864. It was much needed. The rocky north, south and western shores are well littered with at least 27 shipwrecks.

One of the wrecks endowed Robben Island with the aura of a genuine treasure island and gave it a sad little ghost story. In 1693 the Dutch East Indiaman *Goude Buys*, outward bound from the Netherlands with a rich cargo of gold and other valuables for the trading stations in the East, came to grief on the west coast about 24 km north of St Helena Bay. Of the 190 individuals who had set out on the ship, there were fewer than a dozen who had not already died or were in process of dying from scurvy. Leaving the ship at anchor, seven men set off along the shore in search of assistance. Five of these died of hunger; one was found by the local Africans and safely taken to the Dutch East India Company post at Saldanha Bay; the other was eventually rescued after seven weeks of aimless wandering.

The *Goude Buys*, meanwhile, drifted ashore and could not be salvaged. Only one person was found alive in the ship and he died soon after the

rescuers arrived. The cargo, however, could be retrieved. The Cape yacht *Dageraad* was employed on that task. Heavily laden, the yacht, in the misty early hours of 20 January 1694, ran ashore on the western side of Robben Island. Sixteen of the crew drowned while all the salvaged cargo and the treasure scattered among the kelp and rocks. Only fragments have since been retrieved.

Above Robben Island's lighthouse, on Minto Hill, was built in 1864. The light is 47 metres above sea level.

The shipwrecked men were buried on the island. Among them was the skipper, and of him there is an island folk tale. Over his grave is a ship's anchor. It is said that his ghost used to roam about, frightening everyone by its wailing. The anchor was put on the grave to hold down the restless spirit, which was thenceforth allowed to wander only as far away as the anchor cable length. The spirit guards the wreck, sitting on the rocks at night at the scene of the disaster, bewailing the mishap.

In 1913 the lunatics were removed from the island to mainland asylums, and in 1931 the lepers were transferred to Pretoria. After all the years of

and an anti-aircraft battery. Several thousand servicemen – and service-woman – did their wartime duty on Robben Island.

At the end of the war came another era in the story of the island. The South African Navy established a base and training centre for seamen on what they called SAS *Robbeneiland*. During the war and immediate post-war years a one-mile security zone was imposed, which allowed the marine population to flourish. Line fish, abalone and rock lobster increased to at least something like the numbers which must once have found a home in a typical West Coast kelp-bed ecosystem.

MONUMENT AND MUSEUM

In 1960 control of the island passed to the Department of Prisons. A new maximum-security jail was erected and the first political prisoners were sent to the island two years later, by a regime intent on reviving the historic use of the place as a dumping ground for individuals the politicians considered best out of sight and out of mind. The intake included most of the then leadership of the African National Congress, headed by the revered Nelson Mandela. They remained on the island, doing hard labour in such occupations as rock quarrying, until the last of them were transferred to mainland jails on 15 May 1991. About 600 common criminals replaced them.

This dismal period produced one minor compensation. As a maximum-security jail the wildlife of the island and the surrounding sea was stringently protected from the usual depredations of fishermen, treasure seekers and assorted looters of nature. The fish flourished, the bird population increased spectacularly with even mainland birds such as cattle egrets and black-crowned night herons arriving to breed in security. Penguins, locally extinct following which their mass slaughter, made a welcome return. In the 1970s the South African National Foundation for the Conservation of Coastal Birds (SANCCOB) found it convenient to release on the island penguins which they had cleaned of pollution from oil spills. At first the penguins simply used the island as a staging post on their return to their homes on islands such as Dassen, but in 1983, nine breeding pairs made their nests. The colony is now well established.

In 1996 the island was declared a national heritage site and museum. Control passed to the Department of Arts, Culture, Science and Technology. In January 1997 the first parties of tourists visited the island on conducted tours, including the prison and the cell occupied for so long by Nelson Mandela. On 1 December 1999 Robben Island was declared a World Heritage Site by UNESCO.

Visitors to the island catch the ferry from Jetty 1 in the Victoria & Alfred Waterfront. During the 30 minute voyage they enjoy a video showing the history of the island. Tour guides, who are former political prisoners, show guests around the maximum security jail, and then a bus takes them on a

their isolation, it had been found that salt-sea air was actually deleterious to their condition. The wards they had occupied were destroyed by fire. Irishtown went into decline. From a peak population of 2 000 in the 1920s, the place became something like a ghost town. Houses and hospital wards stood empty. A green tangle of vegetation grew over the cemetery. For a time the lighthouse keepers and their families were about the only inhabitants.

Then, with World War II looming, a new activity commenced. The South African Defence Force took over the island and prepared it as a fortress to guard the entrance to Table Bay. Construction work included a harbour at Murray's Bay, an airstrip, emplacements for three large cannon

Above The Robben Island ferry is by far the busiest boat on the Victoria and Alfred Waterfront.

circular trip, stopping at the house where Robert Sobukwe was held, the lime quarry where the political prisoners worked, the Leper Church and several other landmarks before stopping at the village.

FORESHORE AND ADDERLEY

To explore Cape Town it is fitting to start from the docks. The two main dock gates both face Table Mountain from slightly different angles and take the traveller on to what is known as the Foreshore. This is the 145 ha level area reclaimed from the sea during the vast dredging operations which, as mentioned, were necessary for the construction of the Duncan Dock.

When the dredging and pumping were over, Cape Town found itself separated from its harbour by a wide, open, windswept Foreshore which, once the dust had settled, had great potential to provide the city, already compressed between mountain and sea, with a unique face-lift. Today the Foreshore comprises a grid of wide streets and a hotchpotch of buildings. The original anchorage of Roggebaai is buried deep beneath the recla-mation; traversed by the main thoroughfare known as the Heerengracht ('Gentleman's canal'), the name given in former years to the canalised lower section of the Fresh River. The traffic junction of this thoroughfare outside the dock gates is the unmarked beginning of one of the most romantic highways in the world – the Cape-to-Cairo road, followed by countless travellers using many different forms of transport.

Further up the Heerengracht, there is a traffic circle around a fountain and ornamental pools where a happy and garrulous squawk of sea-birds habitually disport themselves. The site of the pools roughly marks the original shoreline. Growing in the vicinity are a few palm trees, displaced relics of a once-handsome row of palms standing along a vanished marine promenade. Looking across the pools at the mountain are the graceful bronze statues of Jan van Riebeeck and his wife Maria, standing very near to the spot where this founder of Cape Town must have been happy to step ashore from his little ship on 7 April 1652.

The statues and pools mark the end of the Foreshore. Among the var-ious buildings standing on it is the Artscape complex, containing an opera house and theatre, both well equipped, with excellent acoustics and seat-ing. Each year many performances of ballet, opera, music, drama and other theatrical entertainments take place at these two venues. Facing this complex is the massive Civic Centre.

Beyond the statues of Van Riebeeck and his wife is the main street of Cape Town, Adderley Street, named after C.B. Adderley, a member of the British House of Commons who, in 1850, gave considerable support to the people of the Cape Colony in their struggle to dissuade the British

Right Visitors to Signal Hill have this panoramic view of city and bay, extending to the cloud-decked Koeberg hills.

Government from turning the colony into a convict settlement. At the beginning of Adderley Street is an imposing bronze monument to those who fell in the two World Wars and the Korean War. It was sculpted by Vernon March, who modelled it on the famous Winged Victory (the Nike of Samothrace) in the Louvre.

On the right-hand side of the street in front of the Medical Centre, just

Above The Castle courtyard is a refuge from the busy life of the city. The gabled arch is the main entrance.

before the war memorial, there is a small bronze ship mounted on a pedestal erected in memory of Robert Falcon Scott, the explorer of the Antarctic. On the left-hand side of the street, opposite the monument, are the extensive buildings housing the Cape Town railway station, airways and coach terminus.

Adderley Street, lined with commercial buildings, leads for nine blocks towards the mountain. It is the city's main shopping thoroughfare and is an animated scene during the week. New arrivals from overseas are immediately aware that there is a peculiar quality to the air in Southern

Africa that seems to make everything a little brighter than it really is. Certainly Adderley Street on a clear morning has an attractive sparkle, with everybody on the run and fast-moving pedestrians and traffic showing an alarming tendency to ignore each other. The pedestrian traffic is interestingly cosmopolitan, a many-hued throng presenting a well-dressed, amiable, perhaps overfed picture, with African ladies flaunting bright colours to particular advantage.

After commercial hours the city area tends to become deserted as Capetonians abandon it for homes and entertainment in the suburbs. Cafés with open doors become hard to find. However, for the young late-night reveller, there is a wide choice of clubs, discos and live music.

The buildings of Adderley Street are attractive, without any particularly noteworthy examples of modern architecture. The railway station is connected to the opposite side of Adderley Street by an underground shopping mall. Between the General Post Office and the railway station there is the extensive Golden Acre development, a massive complex housing shops, restaurants, cinemas and offices on the site of Cape Town's first railway station. The Golden Acre is on the site an early reservoir, built in 1663, the walls of which were salvaged, carefully removed and preserved in the precincts of the new building. At this reservoir, old-time seafarers filled their water casks and bartered for food.

Just up Adderley Street from the Golden Acre, there is a roofed alley known as Trafalgar Place. This is the centre for Cape Town's flower sellers, where loquacious ladies and men of varied temperament offer wonderful blooms for sale, and combine any transaction with a colourful commentary on life in general.

THE CASTLE OF GOOD HOPE

The Grand Parade Centre building and the post office were built on what was originally part of the military parade-ground in front of the castle. It's now, mainly, a parking area with a row of stalls at the western end – site of Van Riebeeck's first earthwork fort. Nothing remains of this. The Castle of Good Hope, which replaced it, was built on the northern end of the parade between 1666 and 1679. In it there is an interesting military museum containing uniforms and medals as well as other items relating to the Cape's military history. The defensive cross wall known as the Kat, built in 1691 across the interior grounds of the Castle, once contained the official quarters of the Governor and his staff. The ornamental balcony in front of the Kat was the scene of important proclamations and the swearing in of new governors. Today the Kat houses a fine collection of paintings, furniture and ceramics of the Cape, known as the William Fehr Collection. The Castle is open to the public; the changing of the guard takes place at 12h00 daily. The ceremony of the keys takes place at 10h10 daily, and re-enacts the ceremonial of the 17th century.

Overlooking the Grand Parade is the City Hall, a massive sandstone building in the Italian style, completed in 1905. The clock tower contains, apart from an excellent clock, the first and largest carillon (44 bells) in South Africa. The hall was the home for several years of the Cape Town Symphony Orchestra, a body of professional musicians giving concerts of a first-class standard often under the baton of international guest conductors. The orchestra is now based at the Artscape Centre and carries on the tradition of good music. It also goes out into the community and plays at venues throughout the Greater Cape Town area.

ADDERLEY STREET TO BO-KAAP

Above the intersection with Darling Street, Adderley Street continues towards the mountain. On the left-hand side stands one of its most notable buildings, the Groote Kerk ('Great church'). This, the mother church of the Dutch Reformed Church is Southern Africa, is also the oldest surviving church, completed in 1704 and enlarged twice since. It contains a magnificent pulpit carved by Anton Anreith.

Beyond the Groote Kerk, on the same side of Adderley Street, stands the old Slave Lodge, originally the quarters for slaves employed in the great vegetable garden founded by Van Riebeeck and maintained by the Dutch East India Company to provide fresh food for ships. In later years, when slavery came to an end, the lodge became the building housing the Supreme Court. Previously known as the South African Cultural History Museum, the Slave Lodge contains an interesting collection of furniture and articles from Cape Town's past. The customs and art of the Islamic people in the Cape are well presented.

Adderley Street ends with the Slave Lodge. A sharp right-hand turn takes traffic into the beginning of Wale Street (Waale or Walloon Street, where two individuals of that nationality used to live), which then climbs the lower slopes of Signal Hill to reach what is known as the Bo-Kaap ('High Cape') or Malay Quarter, an interesting area largely inhabited by Muslims. Many of the neat little cottages here have recently been restored; there are several pretty mosques, and the call to prayer can be heard at all proper hours.

The various annual festivals, such as the Feast of the Orange Leaves held on the birthday of the Prophet (the date varies in the non-Muslim calender) and Ramadan (in the ninth lunar month from new moon to new moon) are all devoutly observed. Weddings, funerals and Tamat (when a Muslim boy completes his study of the Koran) are all practised in the Malay Quarter. One of the restored houses, 71 Wale Street, has been converted into the Bo-Kaap Museum.

Above Cape Town's flower sellers, and their wares, at Trafalgar Place, have been famous for decades.

THE CULTURAL MIX

A very diverse population of human beings made their homes in what become simply known, without formal naming, as Cape Town. Retired soldiers, sailors, time-expired employees of the Dutch East India Company, mercenaries, adventurers and wanderers of many different nationalities made their homes there. A fair sprinkling of retired pirates too, who, having made fortunes from their nefarious trade, 'turned honest' and settled within the blue afternoon shadow of Table Mountain. There were slaves – brown, black and yellow – from Indonesia, Mozambique, Madagascar, and West and East Africa. To communicate with one another, a new language of convenience was created, basically the official Dutch from the Netherlands, but modified by words and pronunciations derived from many other sources. It was a language increasingly spoken first by slaves, farmers and labourers, and then, willy-nilly, by the officials, clergy, traders and aristocrats – the language eventually recognised as Afrikaans.

The culture of Cape Town, predictably, developed as an interesting blend, a major element of which is the irrepressible cheerfulness and joy of living expressed in the Cape Minstrels' Carnival held annually on 1 and

2 January. On these days there is great celebration. The origin of the carnival is uncertain. Some say that it started as an annual reminder of the ending of slavery in the Cape. To others it is simply a colourful way of starting the new year. For several months before the end of the year, groups of individuals form minstrel troupes, each with its own costume, colours, songs and musicians. On the days of the carnival, the troupes pour through the streets of Cape Town and converge on the stadium at Green Point, where they compete with one another in singing, music and colourful costumes that are new every year.

AROUND THE GARDEN

The hospitality of Cape Town was integral with its reputation as the Tavern of the Seas. The descendants of the slaves as well as the freemen and the time-expired soldiers, sailors and officials who chose to remain in the area at the end of their contracts with the Dutch East India Company, created between them a notable industry in the provision of food and good cheer for the passing ships. Farmers, butchers, bakers, vintners and fishermen all worked to contribute to the bill of good fare on offer. To supply the fresh vegetables and fruits so essential for the repair of the ravages of scurvy and malnutrition of long periods at sea, the Company created the great vegetable garden, founded in 1652 and nourished by the same mountain stream which provided good drinking-water. The Company's Garden is now a botanical showcase covering less than 6 ha of the original area, and planted with flowers, trees and shrubs collected from many parts of the world. In this pleasant place there are delightful walks, an open-air tea-room, aviaries, lily ponds and statues of public figures. The bell tower next to the aviary was built in the style of the Cape-Dutch slave bell towers.

The oldest tree in the Garden is a saffron pear (*Pyrus communis*), believed to date from Van Riebeeck's time. The original trunk is dead. The present four arms arose as suckers around the parent. Aloes flower in winter. Demonstrations of rose pruning are given at the end of each July. The various ponds are cleaned in September and surplus goldfish are sold to the public. These fish and a lantern made of white granite were presented to Cape Town in 1932 by Japan as a token of appreciation for kindness shown to Japanese immigrants when passing Cape Town on their way to South America. The sundial bears the date 1787, but its history and it's origin are unknown.

The area of the old Company's Garden steadily diminished over the years as buildings were erected on much of it. Most important of the structures are the South African Houses of Parliament, originally built in 1885 and since much enlarged. Each January the National Assembly commences its sitting with some pomp and ceremony. A second session starts at the beginning of August. In the basement of the Parliament building there is a magnificent library of Africana, the Mendelssohn Library. The grounds and buildings of the Houses of Parliament are immaculately maintained, and there is a graceful statue of Queen Victoria among the trees on the lower side. Guided tours of the Houses of Parliament take place throughout the year .

Immediately across Government Avenue from the terracotta brick Parliament buildings is the sandstone Anglican cathedral of St George the Martyr, designed by Sir Herbert Baker to replace an older cathedral on the same site.

Between the cathedral and the Garden is the building complex of the National Library of South Africa housing a massive collection of books dealing with Africa. Among them is the Grey Collection, donated to the

Left A graceful 19th century memorial fountain in the Company's Garden commemorates an early Cape politician.

library by Sir George Grey, a former governor of the Cape Colony. The collection is housed in the annexe and comprises about 5 000 volumes, including many medieval manuscripts, early printed books and first editions of famous works. There is a first folio Shakespeare (1623), easily the most valuable volume, and a copy of the second folio (1632), as well as a 15th century copy of Dante's *Divine Comedy* and a 14th century copy of Mandeville's *Travels* (in Flemish). The library also contains the oldest book in South Africa, the four Gospels, a manuscript authentically dated about the year 900. The Library is open to the public on weekdays.

Further up Government Avenue, on the same side as the Parliament buildings, stands De Tuyn Huys ('The garden house'), surrounded by beautifully kept formal gardens. Today this is the town residence of the President of South Africa. It was built in 1699 as a pleasure lodge in the Garden for the Governor, Willem Adriaan van der Stel, who used it to escape the confines of his more formal residence in the Castle. Later British governors resided there permanently, and many illustrious guests have graced its spacious rooms.

Government Avenue is itself a renowned feature of Cape Town. It is a fine kilometre-long promenade through a shady tunnel of oak trees inhabited by a permanent population of doves, pigeons and American squirrels (introduced by Cecil Rhodes more than a century ago). All live comfortably on handouts of bread and peanuts from a benevolent public. A discord of vagrant cats lives agreeably on the hand-fed doves, pigeons and an occasional unwary squirrel. A walk through the Avenue, feeding the animals or lolling on the numerous benches, are all pastimes which Capetonians and visitors have enjoyed for many years.

THE ODDBALLS OF THE AVENUE

It is on Government Avenue, too, that the characters of the town, the eccentrics and dropouts, spend much of their time. Such individuals come and go in all cities, and they add a touch of spice to an otherwise staid, humdrum world. Cape Town has known some marvellous and attractively quaint characters among this community of bench sitters and Avenue promenaders. There was old 'Professor' Herbst with his long white beard and seafarer's attire, who sold love potions for a living; there was a woman who wore the same dress every day for years, it is said, to spite her husband who had once accused her of extravagance in buying clothes. Towards the end of her life the dress was an incredible garment made up of threads and patches. Then there was a mystery man, always dressed in knickerbockers and carrying a paper shopping carrier; and a rabbinical character who slept on benches and snored loudly; and a man who lived

Right Tuynhuys was once the residence of English governers, and is now the President's home.

well for years by coaxing plump doves and pigeons into a paper bag containing titbits; and Cape Town Charlie, who earned a living as a snake charmer and conjurer, and many more.

In modern times we had Cas Lucas, a happy-go-lucky individual who claimed to have achieved his life's ambition by becoming Cape Town's top

tramp. A frequently photographed pair were Iris Theodora Holmes and her son Anthony, who, for 48 years, fed the birds and squirrels in the Avenue each day. Around 1980, the reigning characters were a brother-and-sister team, Giesbert and Dagmar Westphal, known locally as the 'Sack People' on account of their strange attire made up of sacks. They

spent their time strolling the streets deep in conversation or sitting on benches in the Avenue, tapping a collection plate with a gentle request to passers-by to give them 'something'. And always there is a new face, a new story among the familiar characters of the Avenue.

GALLERIES AND MUSEUMS

The upper portion of the present Garden is crossed by an open space containing ornamental ponds and a number of statues and monuments of persons and events, the most notable being a memorial to South African soldiers killed in the Battle of Delville Wood during the First World War. On the southeast side of this open space is the South African National Gallery, which exhibits a collection of European and South African art. The European collection includes works representative of the main schools of English and Dutch paintings. Perhaps the best known is Gainsborough's 'Lavinia', and there are good specimens of the work of Raeburn, Reynolds, Romney and Morland. The Dutch pictures include works by Heremans, Vijtmens, Van der Kessel and other 17th and 18th century artists. There are paintings of the 17th and 19th century French schools, and works of such English painters of the early 20th century as Wilson Steer, Sickert, Rothenstein and John. A highlight of the collection is the Sir Abe Bailey Collection of sporting pictures – one of the most distinguished of its kind in the world. It includes paintings and drawings by George Stubbs, Herring senior and junior, James Pollard and Munnings, among others. There is also a collection of leading South African and African artists.

On the opposite side of the open space stand the buildings of the South African Museum which has a notable collection of San rock art, the mysterious Lydenburg Heads, the only example of a quagga foal (the species is extinct) and 250 million-year-old Karoo mammal-like reptiles. The Whale Well with its skeleton of a blue whale is well worth a visit. A planetarium, attached to the main building, presents shows daily including an evening show once a week.

Just above the art gallery loom the twin towers of the Great Synagogue, built in 1905 alongside the original synagogue, the first in South Africa (opened in 1862). The picturesque old synagogue housing the Jewish Museum has now been linked by a walkway to a new specially designed museum building erected behind it. The Cape Town Holocaust Museum, the first and only Holocaust Centre in Africa, stands next door to the Great Synagogue in the Albow Centre in Hatfield Street. It contains a permanent exhibition on the Holocaust, including text and photo panels, archival documents and film footage, multimedia displays, artefacts, recreated environments and survivor testimonies. Both museums are open Sundays to Fridays.

Further along Government Avenue are a pair of ornamental gateways guarded by stone lions (the work of the sculptor Anton Anreith). The gate-ways were once the entrance to a menagerie established by Governor Adriaan van der Stel. A beasts-of-prey park was situated on the right-hand side and a bird and antelope park on the left. The right-hand gateway now leads to a cluster of buildings housing the Michaelis School of Fine Art, the Little Theatre and other cultural and educational institutions, one of which is constructed in neo-Egyptian style. It was built for the South African College (later the University of Cape Town) in 1839 as the city's first building erected for higher education. Near to it is Bertram House, a Georgian brick edifice constructed in the 1830s as a town house and now serving as a museum displaying the British contribution to life at the Cape.

Government Avenue ends where it is bisected by Orange Street. The imposing pillared entrance just across Orange Street leads to the Mount Nelson Hotel with its beautiful grounds, private property for the enjoyment of the hotel's guests.

Besides the main artery of Adderley Street, the city area of Cape Town has many other interesting streets. Plein Street, named after Stal Plein ('Stable square'), is a busy shopping thoroughfare, at the top of which, at the square, there is an equestrian statue of military hero and first Union prime minister Louis Botha, the Roman Catholic Cathedral of St Mary, and the Lodge de Goede Hoop, the first Masonic lodge in South Africa.

St George's, Burg and Long are also commercial streets. Burg bisects Greenmarket Square, the site of the original open-air vegetable market, is now the scene of a fleamarket. On one side stands the attractive Old Town House, built in 1761, originally the Burgher Watch House and later the civic centre and council house of Cape Town. It was replaced by the present city hall in 1905 and is now preserved as a national heritage site housing the Michaelis Collection of old Dutch and Flemish paintings. The pride of the collection is a woman's portrait painted by Frans Hals and probably the most valuable in Southern Africa.

Unfortunately modern buildings have replaced most of the older structures in Cape Town. The few that remain are hemmed in by aggressive new developments. In Strand Street, after it bisects Burg Street, stands a handsome Lutheran church, built surreptitiously in 1774 by Martin Melck, a wealthy Lutheran merchant who erected it ostensibly as a store-room in the days when no religion was tolerated in the Cape other than the Dutch Reformed. The sexton's house adjoining this Lutheran church was built in 1787 and is now occupied by the Netherlands Consulate. On the south side of the church is the Martin Melck House, a fine specimen of an 18th century Cape-Dutch townhouse and now a business centre.

On the opposite side of Strand Street stands another graceful old house, built in 1702 and named the Koopmans-de Wet House after the family who acquired it at the beginning of the 19th century. It is now a historical monument and museum, containing an interesting collection of period furniture, antiques and prints.

TOWARDS THE MOUNTAIN

Between the top of Government Avenue and the slopes of Table Mountain lie the oldest residential suburbs of Cape Town. Gardens is a popular place for boarding-houses and rooms for business people. Vredehoek ('Peaceful corner') and Kloof (cleft) are also populated by working and business people of the city; Oranjezicht ('Orange view'), originally a farm, was so named because the farmhouse had a view of the Oranje bastion of the Castle of the Cape of Good Hope.

Tamboerskloof ('Drummer's ravine') is further west, against the slopes of Lion's Head; Devil's Peak, University Estate and what used to be a picturesquely decrepit slum area, District Six, all lie on the slopes of Devil's Peak. District Six, now demolished, once enjoyed an atmosphere of great vitality and gaiety, despite its conditions of anguished poverty. There are plans to rebuild District Six as a residential area.

The eastern boundaries of the farm on which the suburb of Oranjezicht now stands were along the banks of the Fresh River. Although this river has been forced underground in the lower reaches of its flow through the modern city, the stream in its upper reaches remains on the surface; and, in the winter rainy season when there is a flow of water, it is pleasant to walk along its shady banks and find lingering there something of the atmosphere of Cape Town long ago.

To reach the beginning of this still-unspoilt upper valley of the Fresh River, go up what was once the outlying street of Cape Town, Buitenkant ('Outer side') Street, which passes the lovely old rococo house Rust en Vreugd ('Rest and peace'), now a national heritage site and gallery for fine water-colours collected by William Fehr. Among these paintings are a number by the famous wildlife artist, Edmund Caldwell.

Beyond Rust en Vreugd, the street continues up the hill in the direction of Table Mountain. Passing the Gardens Shopping Centre, one reaches the imposing building and grounds of Highlands House, the Jewish old age home.

It is here that the Fresh River is free from its conduit and flows merrily down the lower mountain slopes through a beautiful, tree-filled valley, nowadays called the Van Riebeeck Park, attractively laid out with picnic spots and shady glades. Many lovely, perfectly maintained homes such as Rheezicht nestle among the trees on both sides of the valley. In former years a cobbled pathway known as the 'slave walk' made its way up this portion of the valley to wash houses where the clothes of Cape Town were laundered.

Further up, on a steep slope of the tongue of land between the river and its tributary stream, stood a house whose ruins, more than half buried

Above A cloudy tablecloth starts to form on the mountain above the city. This is a characteristic of the South-east wind.

ASCENDING THE HEIGHTS

Climbers have found over 350 separate routes, ranging from easy to very difficult, to the summit of Table Mountain. This great pile of sandstone, a mountain playground in the backyard of a city, is also a National Heritage site, National Park and recreational area belonging to all, with wild flowers in astonishing profusion, sizes and colours, ranging from the giant protea to the fragile disa, to be seen somewhere on the mountain throughout the year.

The level but rough and rocky summit has many points of interest. It is 3 km long, east to west, with its highest point, the 1 086 m Maclear's Beacon (Sir Thomas Maclear was a one-time Astronomer Royal), on the eastern end.

The western end of the narrow table plateau supports the distinctive concrete 'pimple' of the upper cable station, where the engines are housed which safely lift over 500 000 people to the summit each year.

The cableway was opened in October 1929 and, notwithstanding many hazards, nobody had been killed in the its construction and no serious accident ever marred its operation. It was replaced with a new cableway in 1997. The upper and lower cable stations were rebuilt to accept larger, circular shaped cable cars, weighing 13 tons each and holding 65 passengers. They are similar to the cable cars used on mountains in Switzerland, and they carry 890 passengers an hour instead of the old 250.

There are two carrying (or track) cables, 1 220 m long and 46,5 mm thick. They have a breaking strain of 168 tons and are minutely inspected once each month. The two cabins counterbalance each other. One goes up as the other goes down, taking about 6 minutes to do the journey. The breaking strain of the hauling rope is over 36 tons. The driving engine is powered by electricity from Cape Town. If the power supply failed, the cabin would remain stationary until an auxiliary power supply was switched on.

The experience of going up the Table Mountain cableway is unique. There is tremendous drama in the great rock mass of the mountain. The cable cars revolve slowly as they travel and the view expands with every metre the car climbs, revealing the whole of Cape Town, with Table Bay and a long view northwards to the mountain ranges on the far horizon. It is always best to check with the cableway office as to whether they are running or not as, often, the wind can come up at short notice. It is also possible to pre-book tickets.

Climbing the mountain by foot and hand should not be attempted without expert advice, as several people are killed on it each year. The Mountain Club of South Africa is happy to advise prospective climbers, and publishes an excellent guide and map for walkers and climbers, with all climbs rated.

The narrow tabletop falls away sharply into the back table, a walker's rugged paradise, with gorges, wild flowers, pine forests, and a set of reservoirs supplying water to Cape Town. This back table eventually ends precipitately in the south in Orange Kloof. Its eastern precipices, beautifully

in shrubbery, still overlook the valley through a tangle of oak and fir trees. The view stretches as far as the distant waters of Table Bay. There are many legends about this house, which was called De Grendel van de Platteklip Kloof ('The bolt of the flat stone cleft') because it blocked access to the upper reaches of the valley. Its isolated situation, the shadows of the trees and the tumbling rush of a waterfall beside it, certainly make it an ideal home for ghosts. Here, legend has it, lived Antjie Somers, the favourite bogeyman (or woman) of the Cape Coloured people. Antjie is a mystical character who appears in many rhymes and tales, especially those told by mothers to frighten naughty children. In this area too, according to folklore, stood Verlatenbosch ('Abandoned bush'), where the leprous son of a former governor lived in solitude. He had apparently

been infected by playing a flute he had picked up, once owned by a leper and deliberately placed by an enemy of the governor where his son could find it. The sound of the flute is said still to haunt the area.

Just above the ruins of the abode of Antjie Somers, the Fresh River comes racing down over a series of flat rock surfaces. These give the name of Platteklip ('Flat stone') to the higher reaches and the great diagonal gorge which cleaves the front of Table Mountain, providing the easiest (but dullest) scramble up to the summit where the busy little river has its source.

Above The cable cars revolve during their short journey between bottom and top.

wooded, overlook the southern suburbs of Cape Town. The twelve sun-drenched and bare buttresses of its western precipices, known as the Twelve Apostles, dominate the Atlantic Ocean suburbs such as Camps Bay.

THE MOUNTAIN'S NEIGHBOURS

The actual western edge of the table, with the upper cable station and restaurant on its top, falls away almost alarmingly to the saddle of land known as Kloof Nek. This saddle links Table Mountain to one of its satel-lites, the 669m high Lion's Head, a striking sugarloaf-shaped peak con-nected by a long body to a rump known as Signal Hill, which overlooks the docks. Signal Hill has on it the ceremonial cannons of Lion's Battery which, by firing a shot at noon each day, prompt the pigeons of Cape Town to take fright and the human populace to check their time. Lion's Head was once known as the Sugarloaf. The reason for the change of name is apparently either its shape, or the shooting there of the last Cape lion. For many years a look-out man was stationed on its summit to warn Cape Town merchants, and the military, with a small signal cannon and flags of the approach and identity of ships.

A well trodden pathway spirals to the summit through sparkling groves of silver trees and lovely spring displays of watsonias, its final stretch up steep rocks facilitated by chains. The climb is not unduly demanding and the 360-degree panorama is, if anything, aesthetically superior to the higher but more directional view from the top of Table Mountain.

The road which climbs the lower slopes of Lion's Head runs past the domed kramat (tomb) of Mohammed Gasan Gaibbie Shah and leads to the summit of Signal Hill. There is a picnic site nearby, on top of the sad-dle of land linking Lion's Head to Signal Hill. A pair of old signal cannons are mounted on a look-out just above the tomb. Countless sightseers have travelled this road to view the scene at night, when the whole city lies glittering like a fairyland necklace elegantly suspended around the smoothly curved neck of Table Bay. Midnight on the last day of the year is a memorable time to be on this wonderful vantage-point. The glow of lights, firing of rockets, distant sounds of revelry, hooting of ships, whistling trains, the sound of bells, all rising from the city and echoing and reflect-ing from the watching face of Table Mountain, provide an almost dream-like prelude to the coming year. Table Mountain is floodlit.

From the Signal Hill observation point it is pleasant to drive back to Kloof Nek and then along Tafelberg Road which, with its constantly chang-ing views, is lovely by day and night. It follows the 350 m contour below the cliffs of Table Mountain, past the lower cable station to the slopes of the 1 001 m high Devil's Peak, which stands guard on the flank of Table Mountain opposite to Lion's Head.

Devil's Peak was originally known as the Wind Mountain. The reason for

Above Lion's Head, to the right of Table Mountain was once called 'The Sugarloaf'.

its two names is not only interesting but also explains several local weath-er peculiarities. An oft-told local legend introduces us to a retired pirate named Van Hunks. This rugged character, it appears, was accustomed to spend his days sitting beneath a clump of trees at what is known as Breakfast Rock on the summit of the saddle of land connecting Devil's Peak to Table Mountain. There he passed his time smoking a potent mixture of rum-soaked tobacco and viewing the shipping in the bay, speculating on the wealth of their cargoes. One day the Devil visited Van Hunks and the two began a smoking contest. This contest continues throughout the summer months. (In winter Van Hunks has rheumatism and cannot climb the mountain.) Proof of the competition is the marvel-lous, billowing, smoke-like cloud which in the summer season seems to begin at the clump of trees at Breakfast Rock, grows, expands and then rolls over the summit of Table Mountain to produce the phenomenon of the table-cloth.

The scientific explanation for the table-cloth is equally fascinating (see page 4), and is closely associated with Cape Town's famous southeast wind. This is the prevailing wind during the summer, appearing towards the end of October and petering out in February, leaving just before the most idyllic months at the Cape, March and April. In May the northwest wind appears, far less venomous in its impact, but the bringer of cool weather and up to 1524 mm of rain during winter, turning the Cape into a green garden.

CHAPTER FOUR

THE CENTRAL PENINSULA

FOR THE TOURIST, THE EXPLORATION OF THE CAPE PENINSULA is one of the most rewarding travel experiences in the world. The Peninsula is strikingly varied, combining scenery that is both dramatic and charming with a piquant atmosphere.

Centuries ago the serenely beautiful hook-like finger of land, with its interesting ocean currents, its marine fauna and its unique scents and flavours, was accepted as a merging place of East, West and the great dividing continent of Africa. For the indigenous wildlife and people of Africa this was the cul-de-sac of their migration routes from north to south. Later, exotic folk from both East and West joined them in a veritable maelstrom of human cultures, activities and aspirations, enriching the ambiance of this most renowned and strategic Cape.

The drive around the Cape Peninsula, starting and ending at the statues of Jan van Riebeeck and his wife, where Adderley Street merges with the Heerengracht, is 143 km long. It requires at least one full day but no day could be better spent. A more agreeable medley of scenes, atmospheres, experiences, aromas, colours, interesting people, stories, myths and legends, it would be difficult to find anywhere else. Let's be off, then, on a journey of discovery from the city to the Cape of Good Hope and then back with our thoughts full of a day never to be forgotten.

One block from Van Riebeeck's statue, down the Heerengracht towards the docks, there is a turn right into Hertzog Boulevard and then up to the interchange which marks the beginning of National Road N2, the coastal highway which connects Cape Town to Durban and the country of the Zulu . Below this elevated dual carriageway (known here as the Eastern Boulevard), the docks and central city area of Cape Town provide a handsome sight. Table Mountain and its companions, Devil's Peak on the left, Lion's Head and Signal Hill to the right, dominate the scene. Immediately to the right of the road is the area once known as District Six. This was a shabby but vibrantly atmospheric home for the poorer folk of the city – until the whole community was summarily driven out of what

Right The main campus of the University of Cape Town is situated on the slopes of Devil's Peak.

they sometimes called 'fairyland'. District Six was levelled to the ground in the name of apartheid. Its population was dispersed to distant areas, where it would be out of sight and out of mind to an uncaring political regime, just like the old days of Robben Island. The area is being rebuilt. After 3 km there is a turn-off to the first of the southern suburbs of the Cape Town metropole ...

WOODSTOCK AND NEIGHBOURS
The heavily built-up suburb of Woodstock was once a pleasant residential area known as Papendorp but in 1881, when the place was granted a village management board, the name Papendorp sounded slightly odd. The majority of its inhabitants, who were all satisfied customers of the local pub, The Woodstock, arranged a change of name in honour of their favourite place of recreation. Whether the social downfall of the neighbourhood dated from this change of name is unknown, but nonetheless Woodstock became thenceforth a lot less select and more congested.

Beyond the turn-off to Woodstock, Eastern Boulevard joins De Waal Drive, which has come around the slopes of Devil's Peak from the upper portion of the city. At this junction the route has reached its highest level and from this point onwards there is generally a distinct reduction in temperature (especially in summer). The road leaves the built-up area below. On the left there is a fine view over the Cape Flats towards the mountain ranges on the near horizon. On the right, beautifully wooded slopes rise upwards to the Peak's jagged summit.

De Waal Drive has been cut into the slopes in finely graded curves, its verges planted with indigenous flowering species which provide many visitors with their first sight of the wonderful flora of Southern Africa. At the junction, the combined roads take on the name of Rhodes Drive, which sweeps down the slopes of Hospital Bend. On the left is the vast complex of Groote Schuur Hospital, the buildings of the Medical School and, in perhaps unfortunate if convenient proximity, a cemetery. This coincidental grouping of interrelated human activities and inactivities should provide motorists with food for thought, but it seems to have little noticeable effect on the local brand of demon drivers. Hospital Bend is a favourite place for accidents. Groote Schuur Hospital was founded in 1932 and became world famous when Professor Chris Barnard performed the first heart transplant operation there on 3 December 1967. The theatre he used for this renowned operation is now an historical monument.

Below the hospital, to the north and east, the unbeautiful city jumble of concrete and bricks gropes upwards as though trying to engulf the unspoilt mountain heights.

The story of the preservation of this lovely area is interesting. The mountain slopes were part of the farm Welgelegen ('Well situated') owned by the Van Reenen family. On this property Sybrandt Mostert had erected (in 1796) a windmill known as Mostert's Mill and this is maintained today in good working order as a national heritage site. In 1891, Cecil Rhodes, Prime Minister of the Cape Colony, then only 38 years of age but

Opposite Indigenous fynbos, including the Protea family, share the mountain slopes with long established but alien pine trees.

master of the Kimberley diamond mines and one of the most powerful financiers in the world, bought the estate and began acquiring control of the mountain slopes all the way to Constantia Nek far to the south. On his death in 1902 this whole area was bequeathed to the people of South Africa. The brooding spirit of a remarkable man is an indefinable presence guarding this legacy from any spoliation.

Beyond Hospital Bend, 5 km from the start of our journey, the N2 road branches off as Settlers Way and begins its long journey along the southern coast, and De Waal Drive undergoes a change of name. As Rhodes Drive, it swings southwards, passing Mostert's Mill on the left, with its four arms held up to embrace the sun and the wind. The mill is open to the public. Close to it a gracefully designed footbridge takes walkers over Rhodes Drive to a path leading beneath the stone pines, which Rhodes introduced to the Cape from their home in Italy. The path leads through their shade and up the slopes of the mountain., where antelope of a number of species graze, eventually reaching the memorial to Rhodes on a site he particularly loved. From here one can see the whole of the Cape Flats from Table Bay on the left to False Bay on the right, from the built-up suburbs below to the mountain ranges on the northern horizon.

The Rhodes memorial was built by public subscription and unveiled on 5 July 1912. It is an impressive work. It was designed by Francis Masey and Sir Herbert Baker, mainly using granite, Rhodes's favourite stone. The centrepiece is the first cast of the famous bronze statue by G.F.Watts: 'Physical Energy', the original of which stands in Hyde Park, London. The statue faces north, where Rhodes dreamed and schemed of so many things. It is set on a granite base at the foot of a granite stairway guarded by bronze lions. At the top of the stairway, in what resembles a Doric temple, there is a bust of Rhodes inscribed with Kipling's words:

Living he was the land and dead
His soul shall be her soul.

Silver trees, proteas and other species of the Cape floral kingdom flourish around the memorial. Stone pines provide shade to the parking area; a tea-room provides refreshment, while paths lead upwards to join the contour path which wanders through the trees high on the slopes of Devil's Peak. The remains of three blockhouses still stand on these slopes, where they were erected by the British during the time of their first occupation of the Cape (1795-1803). This was the period of the French Revolution,

Left The statue of 'Physical Energy' is a centrepiece of the memorial to Cecil Rhodes.
Opposite The silver tree, Leucadendron argenteum, is one of the delights of Table Mountain.

and the British took over in order to control the Cape's strategic situation and prevent the spread of French revolutionary ideas, which were anathema to the conservative English ruling class. The forts, or blockhouses, were small but sturdily built. A number of the cumbersome cannon of the period were dragged with considerable effort to positions of vantage from which it was hoped any invading Frenchmen, along with their ideas of liberty and equality, could be blown away. No onslaught by the French ever occurred.

OBSERVATORY

From the seats below the Rhodes memorial, a site where Rhodes himself was reputedly fond of sitting, there is a panoramic view over the suburbs built on the eastern side of Rhodes Drive and De Waal Drive. To the northeast lies the suburb of Observatory.

In 1821 the British Admiralty established a southern hemisphere branch of the Royal Observatory. The site selected, on the banks of the Liesbeek River, was then pleasantly rural and free from the glare of modern electric lighting. The purpose of the observatory was to set time and longitude. Many important research tasks were also given to this observatory and many distinguished scientists worked in it. Its principal instruments were the 1m Elizabeth reflecting telescope and the 0,6m Victoria refracting telescope. Apart from its observations, the observatory was given the task of setting standard time for Southern Africa; and later, by remote electrical control, it fired the noon gun on Signal Hill.

But the steady encroachment of urban areas, atmospheric pollution and floodlighting prompted the establishment, in 1972, of a new observatory near Sutherland in the Karoo, where the skies are unpolluted and, for much of the year, unaffected by clouds. The main instruments from the Cape Town, Johannesburg and Pretoria observatories were moved to the site. The Royal Observatory in Cape Town remains the administrative centre. The astronomical staff spend about one week in every six at Sutherland, the rest of the time in Cape Town analysing their data and preparing new programmes. Much routine and technical service activity, as well as the measurement of stellar distances, continues in the old Royal Observatory. Guided tours are organised on the second Saturday evening of each month (weather permitting).

MOWBRAY TO RONDEBOSCH

South of Observatory lies the suburb of Mowbray which, like Woodstock, grew up around a roadside tavern, though it began life with a different and much more gruesome name. In 1724 Johannes Beck decided to build a wayside hostelry, and while it was under construction, three slaves, in vengeance for some grievance, murdered a farm foreman named Behr and his wife on a farm close by. It is said that a baby of the murdered cou-

ple survived when its slave nurse hid the infant in the kitchen oven. The slaves were captured, condemned and executed in the usual barbarous manner. They were first broken on the wheel, then beheaded with their heads exhibited on stakes at the scene of the crime. The name Drie Koppen ('Three heads') was attached to the tavern, with a signboard displaying the heads, and the name was passed on to the village which grew around it. Much later the name was changed to Mowbray, the name of a local estate owned by a man from Melton Mowbray in England. The three heads were still depicted on the coat of arms of the municipality which was established in 1890. Three cups, presumably in memory of rollicking times in the tavern, were also included in this rather odd emblem.

Above Rondebosch Common, set beneath jagged Devil's Peak, was once a military camp-ground.

South of Mowbray and immediately east of the Rhodes Memorial is the suburb of Rosebank, much used as a dormitory area for students of the University of Cape Town. In Cecil Road you'll find the Irma Stern Museum, devoted to the work of that outstanding South African artist. The attractive Baxter Theatre complex, part of the University of Cape Town, stands on Main Road.

Originally named Ronde Doorn Bosjen ('Round thorn bushes'), after a long-vanished landmark – a circle of thorn trees – Rondebosch is now covered with attractive residences, schools such as the Diocesan College (Bishops), Rondebosch Boys (high and primary), Westerford (high), Rustenburg Girls Junior and High, in whose grounds stand the original summer residence of the Dutch governors (hence the name, which means 'Place of Rest'). Rondebosch Common, a large open space much used as a camping ground by the Dutch and British military during the long

drawn -out Napoleonic wars, is now a protected space graced by several species of wild flowers. Overlooking it on the eastern side is the Red Cross War Memorial Children's Hospital. In the centre of Rondebosch stands a cast-iron fountain built about 1884 as a drinking trough for horses and which later became the support for the first electrically generated street light in Cape Town.

Rhodes Drive continues from Mostert's Mill, passing (on the right) the creeper-covered walls of the main cluster of University buildings. They are magnificently situated, with the serrated summit of Devil's Peak and the rugged cliffs of the back of Table Mountain forming a backdrop.

A statue of Rhodes, a great benefactor of the place, sits on the steps in front of the university, looking in pensive mood at the playing fields and beyond. The imposing site is on Rhodes's gift of his Groote Schuur estate. The University of Cape Town is the oldest in Southern Africa. It had its

origin in 1829 as a private enterprise named the South African College, housed in the city area. The college became a public venture in 1837 and then, as a university, was transferred to its present situation in 1925, when the foundation stone of the first building was laid by the Prince of Wales, later King Edward VIII.

On the left stands the one-time summer-house of the British governors, known as The Belvedere. Beyond it the dual carriageway curves around the end of the university campus and passes, on the left, the gateway leading to the lovely homestead of Groote Schuur ('Great barn'). This was originally built by Jan van Riebeeck as a grain store. It was converted by later English owners into a residence called The Grange, and then purchased by Rhodes as the nucleus of his great estate along the slopes at the back of Table Mountain and Devil's Peak. A disastrous fire practically destroyed the house in 1896. It was then remodelled for Rhodes in the

Cape-Dutch style by the famous architect, Sir Herbert Baker. From the fire-blackened ruins rose the stately Groote Schuur manor-house of today. It is full of treasures, for Rhodes was a great collector of antiques and curiosities. The garden outside became famous for its hydrangeas, passion flowers and plumbago, all planted in great banked masses which he felt were appropriate to the prodigious scale of the African continent. A pleasant tradition was that each Christmas the hydrangeas were cut, and taken, literally by the truckload, to decorate the wards of Groote Schuur and other hospitals.

Rhodes bequeathed his home as the official residence of the Prime Minister of the Cape (later South Africa). He also built a second house on the estate, The Woolsack, as a summer home for his friend, Rudyard Kipling. This later became the official residence of the Deputy Prime Minister, and is now part of the university. Across the way from Groote

Schuur is Westbrooke, originally bought (in the early 1800s) by Judge William Westbrooke Burton and today the country residence of the State President. The name was changed in 1995 to Genadendal ('the dale or valley of grace').

LADY ANNE'S WORLD

Just beyond the entrance to Groote Schuur, the road reaches the Princess Anne traffic interchange. From here there is a branch leading right to the Rhodes Memorial and to the University of Cape Town. To the east (left) there is a turn leading down to Rondebosch and to Newlands Avenue which takes you beneath a fine avenue of oak trees, past the South African College Schools and through the northwestern side of the suburb of Newlands, one of the choicest of the city's residential suburbs.

From the Princess Anne traffic interchange Rhodes Drive changes its name to Union Avenue and provides a splendid drive with the forest-covered mountain slopes dominating it on the right-hand side. The verges and central islands of the road are lineal gardens of indigenous flowers, while the attractive houses of Newlands drowse their days away in the shade of trees on the left. There is a turn-off to a picnic and barbecue site just after the interchange. At intervals along the length of the forest are parking places, marking the start of paths which wander to many parts of this lovely domain of trees.

In 1706 a part of this forest was granted to Willem ten Damme, who succeeded his father as chief surgeon to the Dutch East India Company in the Cape. He named his possession Paradijs, and built a cottage as a farmhouse, close to a perennial mountain stream flowing down into a deep valley known as De Hel ('The abyss'). It was to this 'paradise' amidst the trees that there came, for a little while, one of the more romantic couples in the Cape story. In 1797, when the British occupied the Cape for the first time, they sent out as governor an Irish gentleman, George Earl Macartney, recently raised to the peerage as reward for many years of diligent service to the British as an ambassador and governor. His wife declined to accompany him to the Cape but amongst the staff he brought with him from England was Andrew Barnard, appointed to the position of Colonial Secretary. Barnard brought with him his wife Lady Anne, daughter of the Earl of Balcarres. She took over the duties of the first lady of the British administration, charged with the organising of social functions and the making of friends with the Kapenaars (Cape people). With her husband she was allotted the Castle Residency for accommodation. This she furnished with tasteful informality. In the Council Room of the castle she held drawing-room receptions and dances with a band of six black fiddlers.

Above This whimsically shaped pool at Kirstenbosch was built in the 19th century by Colonel Bird.

Lady Anne's personal history was interesting. Born in 1750, she was an artist of repute and author of the famous ballad 'Auld Robin Grey'. She became involved in an unfortunate and lengthy love affair with Henry Dundas (later Viscount Melville, Secretary for War and the Colonies). His political ambitions required that he form an alliance with another powerful family, and Lady Anne became something of an embarrassment. She was intelligent, attractive and artistic but at 43 years of age she was still dreaming of an impossible marriage to her lover. There must have been a great deal of hard talking behind the scenes.

The upshot was that Lady Anne was married off to Andrew Barnard, a man thirteen years her junior with little hope of professional advancement without influential friends. What he got was Lady Anne and the appointment to Lord Macartney's staff as Colonial Secretary, a plum job for so young a man. So off he sailed with his talented wife, many horizons away from Henry Dundas, to Cape Town.

The Barnards enjoyed a good living in the Cape. Barnard proved efficient in his position and Lady Anne was a brilliant success as first lady of the administration. The Cape benefited from their presence. Lady Anne endeared herself not only to contemporary local society but also to posterity, through a sequence of letters she wrote to Henry Dundas, recording an amusing, perceptive and most readable picture of life in Cape Town. As a rural escape from their official duties, Lady Anne and her husband were allocated the cottage in the woodlands of Paradijs estate. They found the cottage 'too old and crazy to be safe any longer' (as Lady Anne described it). Barnard therefore set to work and built a 'wee cottage' on an 8-ha plot on the banks of the Liesbeek River. This estate the Barnards named 'The Vineyard'. They moved there in 1800 and spent their spare

Above The Vineyard Hotel enjoys the same view that delighted Lady Anne Barnard.

time in creating a dream garden, digging out the palmiet reeds and planting fruit trees and vegetables. The pity was that time was short. There were changes in the Cape colonial hierarchy, and Lady Anne returned to Britain at the beginning of 1802, never to come back.

The Vineyard at first was abandoned to dilapidation. Then the Governor, Lord Charles Somerset, restored the place as his country retreat. Later it passed into private hands. Fruit, grapes, flowers and vegetables, with pumpkins described as 'big as a barrel of beef' were grown there. Then it became a hotel. The house was enlarged and new buildings constructed but in some indefinable way the amiable, hospitable and romantic personalities of the Barnards remain attached to it. The proud owner of The Vineyard today, has carefully maintained its atmosphere and has preserved within the body of the place something of the elegance and charm of bygone days. The garden is superb, the river still flows along the boundary, while the hospitality is a legacy from Lady Anne.

BEER AND CONVICTS

The pleasant climate, fertility and plentiful fresh water from rainfall, mountain streams and springs not only attracted residents, but provided Newlands with a commercial property of considerable value. The possibilities of reticulating the pure water for domestic use and for the production of aerated drinks and beer were obvious.

Jacob Letterstedt, a Swedish merchant who settled in the Cape in 1822, entered the brewery business. In 1840 Letterstedt built a new mill, with a huge cast-iron water wheel, which he named the Josephine Mill after Crown Princess Josephine of Sweden. Things went well for him until a problem started to develop in the late 1840s. The British Government, in May 1841, proposed that Europeans condemned to long terms of imprisonment in India, particularly soldiers, be sent to Robben Island and, after serving their sentence, be liberated in Cape Town.

There was a public outcry in Cape Town. But the British government seemed obsessed with the idea of clearing out their crowded jails of surplus individuals and proposed various other schemes, which they always withdrew when the local people reacted. The controversy seemed to be dying down. But then, in March 1849, news reached Cape Town that, without further consideration of local feelings, a ship, the *Neptune*, had sailed from Britain with a load of convicts from Pentonville prison, some of them Irishmen serving sentences for trifling offences committed during the potato famine. They were certainly not hardened criminals but the Cape people still wanted none of them.

There was a considerable public disturbance. An anti-Convict association organised a pledge declaring that the undersigned inhabitants of the Cape of Good Hope would not employ or knowingly admit, provide work for, assist, associate with or support convicted felons. Petitions to the Queen, parliament and the people of England were drawn up. The country people supported the town people in a united opposition to the Cape as a convict settlement. Nevertheless, on 19 September 1849 the good ship *Neptune* anchored in Simon's Bay with 282 convicts on board. Mass public meetings were held in Greenmarket Square and on the Grand Parade. The Governor, Sir Harry Smith, was informed that any person, company or government department in any way supplying the *Neptune* would be boycotted.

Weeks passed with the unfortunate ship lying at anchor and nobody allowed to land. On 10 October the names were published in the press of twelve men who were denounced as supplying provisions and aid for the ship. Among these names was that of Jacob Letterstedt. He found his businesses boycotted, and he was (with others) personally assaulted, abused, threatened, his effigy burned and his business premises damaged. The whole dismal affair dragged on until a dispatch from Earl Grey reached Cape Town in February 1850 instructing the Governor to send the *Neptune* on to Van Diemen's Land (Tasmania). There the convicts would receive pardon and be liberated. There was jubilation in the Cape. The ship was provisioned, a small sum of money collected to be given to the convicts, and the *Neptune* sailed away after five dreary months at anchor.

Cape Town relaxed. The principal street, the Heerengracht, was renamed in gratitude after C.B. Adderley, a member of the House of Commons who had ably championed the cause of the Cape in Britain. Those individuals who had supported the government, especially the twelve men who had been denounced in the press and suffered losses by boycott, damage or physical violence, attempted to get some compensation. One of them, Captain Robert Stanford, was knighted for his services in breaking the boycott of supplies and received £5 000, but the rest received nothing. Jacob Letterstedt was particularly aggrieved at the ingratitude of the authorities. He felt that he had supported a government which did not support him. He decided to quit the Cape and move to France.

Letterstedt's Josephine Mill and his brewery in Newlands were eventually sold to Ole Anders Ohlsson, a Swede who had emigrated to the Cape in 1860 and who built the business up into the largest manufacturing enterprise in South Africa.

Newlands is still a supplier of water to the southern suburbs of Cape Town. The springs near the brewery (now owned by South African Breweries) are still used. One of them, the Albion springs, was for long the basis of the softdrinks bottled there by Schweppes until they moved elsewhere.

The Josephine Mill was restored. A fully operational milling museum was incorporated into the building and this is open to the public. The commodious building is also used for concerts. The museum of the South African Rugby Board is housed at the Sports Science Institute, opposite the mill. The entrance to the Newlands rugby ground, home of the Western Province Rugby Union, is close to the mill, with the playing fields of the Western Province Cricket Club and the Kelvin Grove Sports Club on the eastern side of the suburban railway line. Ohlssons Brewery stands across the road from the Josephine Mill.

Union Avenue continues its pleasant way between forest and suburb and then, with a turn eastwards, reaches a crossroads 9,5 km from the

Left Like spectators at a show, the carved wooden faces of Africa gaze back at tourists.
Opposite Cape Town's elegant Italianate City Hall overlooks the Grand Parade and its market stalls.

At the important intersection of Union Avenue with Newlands Avenue and Paradise Road (9,5 km from the city), turn sharp right off the double carriageway and follow the continuation of Rhodes Drive up the avenue (now called Rhodes Avenue) along the bottom of the slopes at the back of Table Mountain. The road is a scenic delight and leads through what is without doubt one of the most attractive residential areas to be found anywhere in the world – the green and fertile expanse of the lands of Van Riebeeck's old farm Boschheuwel ('Bushy hill'), now known more generally as Bishopscourt, after the official residence there of the Anglican archbishop of Cape Town.

Boschheuwel was laid out in the sheltered valley of the upper Liesbeek River. The southeastern rise took the name of Wynberg from Van Riebeeck's farm vineyard. The valley is now covered with lovely homes, and a drive through the estate is a thoroughly enjoyable diversion from the main route of Rhodes Avenue. An especially pleasant little road to explore is Boshof Avenue, the first turn-off to the right down Paradise Road. It passes through the gates of the old Boshof Estate, shaded by a fine avenue of oaks, and continues past many a handsome home including, on the right, the original Boshof homestead with the date 1776 on its gable. Further on is the beautiful and secluded Fernwood (now simply the pavilion of the Parliamentary sports club). In its commodious grounds is contained what is surely one of the most delightful cricket fields to be found anywhere that the game is played.

After 2 km Rhodes Avenue passes the entrance to Kirstenbosch, one of the most famous botanical gardens in the world. In 1811 the area of the future garden became the property of Henry Alexander, the Colonial Secretary in the British administration. He was quite an individualist. He built a homestead with windowless bedrooms, as he considered such rooms would only be used at night. This interesting establishment was unfortunately burned down. Another intriguing construction in 1811 was the exquisite sunken bath in one of the springs of the Liesbeek River. It was built by a Colonel Christopher Bird, in the shape of a bird, and became known as Lady Anne Barnard's Bath in memory of that notable lady. Some visitor started the custom of throwing a coin into the bath and making a silent wish to Lady Anne. The men who service this bath of crystal-clear spring-water appreciate the custom.

Cecil Rhodes bought the whole of Kirstenbosch in 1895 and presented it to the people of South Africa with the intention that it become the site of a botanical garden. In 1911 Professor Harold Pearson confirmed its suitability, and in 1913 it was proclaimed as the Kirstenbosch National Botanical

start of our journey. To the left Newlands Avenue leads through lines of oak trees. Ahead, Union Avenue changes its name for a short distance to Paradise Road. It bridges over the Liesbeek River and then divides into Protea Road, which leads eastwards as a boundary between Newlands and the suburb of Claremont. The other branch, known as Edinburgh Drive, twists southwards, climbs Wynberg Hill past Bishopscourt on the right and then down the southern slopes, with the suburb of Wynberg on the left. Constantia lies on the right, while ahead is a distant view of False Bay and the end of the Cape Peninsula.

CLAREMONT AND KIRSTENBOSCH

Claremont, which has an important commercial centre, is still sometimes referred to as the 'village' and its rugby team is known as the Villagers. But today it is more like an infant city, with a major shopping centre and one

of the most beautiful public parks in Southern Africa, the Arderne Gardens. The garden was originally part of the estate known as The Hill, in the halcyon days when Claremont was still a village in the centre of a quiet rural area. In 1840 an English immigrant, Ralph Arderne, acquired this estate. He was a lover of trees, and on the site he planted one of the finest tree collections in Southern Africa. He acquired about 325 species from all over the world, including magnificent Norfolk Island pines, Indian rubber trees, Atlas Mountain cedars, North American swamp cypresses and many others. All flourished. The Black River has its source here; the spring was converted by Arderne into a delightful Japanese garden with bridges, ferns and water-fowl. Azaleas, rhododendrons and roses grow to perfec-

Above A cool dell at Kirstenbosch where all plants are indigenous to South Africa.

Opposite Spring at Kirstenbosch is the season for bright displays of flowering annuals.

Gardens. Professor Pearson became its first director. The garden encompassed an area of 497 hectares, including the entire overlooking slopes and back summit of Table Mountain right up to the highest point, Maclear's Beacon (1 066 m). In this virgin area Pearson set to work to make a home for the collection, preservation and study of the indigenous flora of Southern Africa. The success of his efforts is gloriously self-evident. Over 4 000 of the 18 000 species of the flora of Southern Africa are happily gathered there with an all-year-round display of flowers amidst a magnificent collection of shrubs, plants and trees. Pearson died in 1916. His grave in the garden has a fitting epitaph: 'All ye who seek his monument look around.'

Pearson's successor was Professor R.H.Compton who, from 1919 to 1953, carefully guided the garden until it became one of the world's principal botanical showcases. The headquarters and shop of the Botanical Society of South Africa are in the gardens. The Compton Herbarium provides an ultimate authority in the identification and classification of the flora of Southern Africa.

INTO THE CONSTANTIA VALLEY

From Kirstenbosch, Rhodes Avenue climbs the southern slopes of the Liesbeek Valley, providing changing views of the fashionable residential area of Bishopscourt. Reaching the top of the slope, it swings sharply right over the Boschheuwel at the junction with Klaassens Road which leads eastwards through the trees to the suburb of Wynberg. A portion of Van Riebeeck's hedge of wild almonds still flourishes on the left-hand side of the road. The route winds through an avenue of chestnut trees, which give way to a lovely tunnel formed by oak trees. This area was acquired by Cecil Rhodes in order to preserve its beauty and to build a scenic drive around the mountain slopes above the estate Bel Ombre all the way to Constantia Nek. The forest above the road is named Cecilia, and through it meander several paths and tracks leading to such beauty spots as the Cecilia Waterfall, and up to the reservoirs on the back of Table Mountain.

Rhodes Avenue continues its way and 5 km from its beginning reaches the end of its journey at the traffic circle on the summit of the divide over Constantia Nek. The avenue merges there with the road from Constantia to Hout Bay. The road to Hout Bay descends through an avenue of oaks while on the eastern side the road makes a curving descent to the green and pleasant area of Constantia. It is this road which we will follow.

Half a kilometre down the eastern side from the summit of Constantia Nek, the main road passes on its left side a bus stop at a small parking place. From here there is a fine walk down the tree-covered valley known

Left Vineyards at Constantia are sheltered by the mountain spine of the Cape Peninsula.

as De Hel ('The abyss'). This circular path, down one side of the valley, crosses the stream at its bottom and back on the far side has rewarded countless walkers with the moderately strenuous pleasure of exploring an unspoilt example of a Cape ravine forest surviving from the past.

From the parking place at De Hel, the main road continues its curving descent through the tall trees. The road is now descending the southeast slopes of the mountain ridge of the Cape Peninsula and passing through the estate of Witteboomen ('Silver trees'). The area has had a succession of owners since Lambert Symonsz bought it in 1697, and the record of sales makes interesting reading. At the one held in 1833 the slaves were the first to be sold. The most valuable, Abraham, a blacksmith, fetched 2 000 rixdollars. Neptune, a Mozambican slave had absconded but was sold in absentia, with the buyer gambling on his apprehension. Ontang, from Batavia, asked if he could buy his own freedom. This was allowed. Nobody else bid for him as he was very old, so he bought himself for four stuyvers (about two cents).

The main road we are following passes, at one point, between the estates of Silverhurst on the left and High Constantia on the right. High Constantia has an imposing manor-house of a design rather surprising to see in an area so essentially associated with Cape-Dutch architecture. The building looks as though it belongs to an illustration to a Walter Scott novel. Its occupants are just as unusual in this setting of vineyards and cellars, for High Constantia is the home in the Cape of the religious order of the Schoenstatt Sisters of Mercy, founded in Germany in 1914 by Father Joseph Kentenich. This lay movement was dedicated to Mary, the Mother of Christ. Members are active in professions, working as doctors, social workers, teachers and nurses. The movement has retreats, and retirement and holiday homes for its members in several parts of the world.

High Constantia also passed through the hands of a succession of owners. Originally the place consisted of a simple thatched house, but in 1902 it was sold to Robertson Fuller Bertram, who had made a fortune on the Witwatersrand gold-fields as a stockbroker, speculative land owner and developer. The suburb of Bertrams in Johannesburg is named after him. Bertram planned to retire at High Constantia and he intended to do it in style. First of all he set out to rebuild the farmhouse, but it fell to pieces. The only thing was to pull it down. The new manor-house was planned on sumptuous lines. Money was no object. There was granite from Scotland, English oak, with a grand staircase carved in England and dominating an entrance hall fit for the reception of a king.

The Bertrams entertained celebrities and aristocrats. The Prince of Wales once danced all night there. Musicians, actors and actresses

Right A sugar bird is among the many species that feed on insects and nectar found on proteas.

enjoyed the Constantia hospitality. Because the guests were such a thirsty lot, Bertram is said to have decided to start making his own wine and, in association with a professional wine-maker, Walter Stokes, he founded Bertrams Wines, producing a variety of alcoholic drinks, including liqueurs such as the traditional Van der Hum.

Where did all the fine wines and glamorous guests go, and the fortune made on the Witwatersrand? Bertram went bankrupt. It was a classic case of the dread Constantia Blight. He died a very sad man in 1942. His wife and son died shortly afterwards. High Constantia fell under the auctioneer's hammer but the imposing mansion was difficult to sell. The farmlands were separated from the house and sold in sections. Somebody tried to turn the house into a hotel but the building wasn't too suitable for the purpose. The usual quick succession of owners followed. Then, in 1957 it was sold to the Schoenstadt Sisters of Mary, who remain there today in this idyllic setting.

The estate opposite High Constantia, on the main road, was originally named Frankengift, then changed to New Constantia and, finally, to Silverhurst because of the silver trees growing there. On this residentail estate memories of the wine-making past linger on. The slave bell dated 1815 stands quiet but remindful of the labours of the past. Across the main road from the entrance to Silverhurst, 3 km from the divide where Rhodes Avenue ended, there is a small cluster of shops, including an outdoor-restaurant. From here a short approach road leads to the manor-house of the estate of Groot Constantia, home to the renowned governor Simon van der Stel.

GROOT CONSTANTIA

The story has been told, in Chapter 2, of the beginning of this estate and of its fragmentation when Van der Stel died in 1712. In 1778 Hendrik Cloete of Nooitgedacht farm in Stellenbosch bought the portion on which stood the manor-house and gave it to his son, also named Hendrik. The Cloete family, who have been so intimately a part of the history of Constantia, came to the Cape with Jan van Riebeeck. Jacob Cloeten was a mercenary soldier from Cologne in Germany; in the Cape they became known by the name of Cloete.

The new owner of Constantia found the place half in ruin, and set to work with a will on restoration. A handsome new cellar was built, said to have been designed by the French architect, Louis Thibault. The sculptor, Anton Anreith, a friend of Cloete, gave him as a gift the famous pediment. The manor-house was almost completely rebuilt, converted from a double-storeyed building to its Cape Dutch style elegance of today. The vine-

Above Constantia harvest: destined to make the wine that once consoled Napolean.

yard had been as much neglected as the house. Cloete planted 10 000 new vines and launched a search for the ideal cultivar for the area. A relative of Cloete, Johannes Colyn, had married a widow who owned De Hoop op Constantia ('The Hope of Constantia'), a fragment of the original estate. Colyn had already begun a systematic testing of each of the soil types and climatic micro-areas on this property. He and Cloete shared results, and the same ambition to establish the Constantia area as a world leader in wine. They succeeded brilliantly, producing on their sections of the original estate two of the most celebrated of all wines – the legendary red and white Constantias.

The two men left posterity no details of the making of these wines. Laboratory tests of the contents of a few surviving bottles found in the cellars of such collectors as the Duke of Northumberland reveal that it was a natural, unfortified wine, the flavour that of a luscious raisin-like liqueur with a subtle aroma. The two wines were a drink for the gods as well as for ordinary mortals. They were carried all over the world, and eulogised in the writings of many celebrated authors. Charles Dickens wrote in *The Mystery of Edwin Drood* of 'the support embodied in a glass of Constantia and a home made biscuit'. Jane Austen in *Sense and Sensibility* advised her heroine Elinor Dashwood to try a glass of Constantia for it had 'healing powers on a disappointed heart'. Alexander Dumas and Henry Longfellow and many others wrote fondly of these wines. Baudelaire, in his poem 'Les Fleurs du Mal' wrote 'Even more than Constantia, than opium, than Nuits I prefer the elixir of your mouth'. They were sipped with appreciation by the captains and the kings. Princess Alice of Athlone liked to reminisce that her grandmother, Queen Victoria, drank a man-sized glass of Constantia wine every evening after dinner. Frederick the Great, Bismarck, the kings of Holland, France and England drank the wine and beguiled their guests at state banquets with its taste and fragrance.

Napoleon, in his exile on St Helena Island, found solace in drinking a bottle a day. On his deathbed, it is reputed that the last thing he asked for was a glass of Constantia.

Strangely enough, the production of this and other wines was made possible in the Cape by the presence over the vineyards of a remarkable bird. Each year in November the steppe buzzards of Russia escape the approaching Siberian winter by migrating across Africa to the Cape. Until the end of March these raptors keep guard over the Cape vineyards, gliding, wheeling and coursing incessantly, killing or driving away fruit-eating birds such as the starlings which are capable of destroying an entire harvest. The buzzards do not eat grapes themselves. By the time they return to Siberia, the grapes have been safely harvested and the wine is maturing in the cellars.

What happened to the two Constantia wines, the most celebrated wines ever made in Southern Africa? Henry Cloete, fourth generation of the Cloetes to own Groot Constantia, was not much interested in a farming life. He liked France and spent most of his time there. He returned to Groot Constantia in 1885 to find the estate in ruins, with the vineyards destroyed by the fungal disease oidium and the root parasite phylloxera. He sold the farm at a public auction. It was bought by the Cape government and converted to a training and experimental farm under the direction of a German viticulturist, Baron Carl von Babo, who knew nothing of the two celebrated old wines. The South African government took over the estate in the early 1960s. In 1976 the estate was transferred to the Groot Constantia Control Board who, although still government owned, ran it as a viable commercial wine producer.

In 1993 ownership of the estate was again transferred, this time from the government to the Groot Constantia Trust. Today, a range of fourteen estate wines are produced and sold *in situ*; tours of the cellar are conducted each hour on the hour between 10h00 and 16h00. The historic farmyard, which includes the famous manor-house, the Jonkershuis complex and the beautiful Cloete cellar, is open to visitors. Some leisurely walks under oak-lined avenues may be enjoyed with a lovely ornamented bath a short walk from the main house. Furthermore the estate offers two restaurants where the wines may be enjoyed as a pleasant accompaniment to good food, including traditional Cape cuisine. Vineyards have been established to produce the famed Constantia wines of yesteryear.

ALPHEN AND THE REMARKABLE JAMES BARRY

From the entrance to Groot Constantia, the main road continues through the residential area, past the Constantia Village shopping centre and, after

Opposite Groot Constantia homestead is one of the classics of gabled Cape Dutch architecture.

3 km, reaches the Alphen interchange with the Simon van der Stel freeway. Just before this interchange there is a turn left onto the Alphen road which leads past the Alphen Hotel, one of the finest and most elegant of South African hostelries.

This area was originally the Alphen farm whose manor-house, built in 1753 by Abraham Leever (known as 'the Monsieur from Amsterdam'), is in the Cape Dutch style but unusual in that it is double-storeyed, the upper floor supported on massive walls, insulating it from the extremes of heat and cold. Tall windows and high-beamed ceilings ensure ventilation from the winds of the Cape. The front and rear parts of the house are divided by a superb screen of yellowwood and stinkwood. The teak front door has elegant baroque arhitecture. The house faces a large oak-shaded square with, on its sides, two cellars in Cape-Dutch style, a Victorian double-storey block known as the Dower House, and the Jonkershuis, which now houses an atmospheric pub.

In 1801 Alphen was bought by Thomas Frederick Dreyer, a great friend of Lord Charles Somerset, Governor of the Cape. Lord Charles and Mr Dreyer were lovers of horses and hunting. Alphen became the base for the Constantia Hunt, complete with all its social trimmings of balls, dinners and entertainments. The Governor was a frequent visitor to Alphen and with him came that remarkable and enigmatic individual, Dr James Miranda Stuart Barry, whose portrait, a copy of the only one known, graces the sitting room at Alphen today.

Dr Barry was born around 1790 of unknown parentage. He was brought up by two individuals he always referred to as his uncle and aunt, the Royal Academician James Barry and his sister Mrs Mary Anne Bulkerley. James Barry died in 1806, a distinguished artist. Two of his patrons, General Francisco de Miranda and David Stuart Erskine, the Earl of Buchan, took an interest in the youth and in 1809 Mrs Bulkerley took him to Edinburgh, where he entered the university and studied medicine, graduating as a doctor in 1812. His thesis was dedicated to his two patrons.

In October 1812, young Dr Barry entered the United Hospitals (Guys and St Thomas's) in London and there qualified as a regimental surgeon. In this capacity he served in Plymouth and London and then was posted to Cape Town, arriving there on 1 August 1816 at the beginning of a remarkable career. Lord Charles Somerset was the Governor of the Cape at that time and Barry had a letter of introduction to him from the Earl of Buchan. Barry, apart from his regimental duties, was appointed physician to the Governor's family.

In appearance Dr Barry was small in stature, red haired with a rather high-pitched voice, prominent eyes, no hair on face and hands, and a notably effeminate disposition, manner, appearance and gait. There were rumours that he was really a female but, of whatever sex, there was no doubting the competence of the individual as a surgeon. In 1819 Barry was ordered to Mauritius to deal with an epidemic of cholera. Back in the Cape in 1822 he was appointed colonial medical inspector. On 25 July 1826 he made medical history when he delivered the wife of T.C. Munnik of a son by the first successful Caesarean operation in Southern Africa. The grateful parents named their son James Barry Munnik. Years later these three names were given as Christian names to a godson of James Barry Munnik. This infant, James Barry Munnik Hertzog, became prime minister of South Africa.

Dr Barry could be brusque and even offensive in his speech. He made enemies of powerful officials by his insistence on more humane treatment of convicts, lepers and the outcasts on Robben Island and the old leper colony at Hemel-en-Aarde. He stopped unqualified persons from acting as doctors and clashed several times with the authorities over the appalling conditions in the Cape Town jail. In June 1824 placards were posted overnight in the streets alleging an unnatural relationship between Dr Barry and the Governor. Notwithstanding the offer of a reward of 5 000 rixdollars nobody was apprehended for the scurrilous attack.

Dr Barry regarded Alphen as something of a home from home and he showed considerable interest in one of the winsome daughters of Mr Dreyer, who had fourteen children. Josias Cloete was also attracted by the young lady and the two fought a formal duel over her on the back steps of the manor-house. Neither of the contestants was injured. They shook hands and became the firmest of friends. What Miss Dreyer thought of the proceedings it would be interesting to know. Barry continued his career at the Cape. The feud with the authorities became more bitter. In 1824 he found a man named Elliot in the jail, lying filthy and verminous, without bed, pillows, blankets or any comfort, and with a broken leg. When the jailer was asked if there were any other prisoners with broken bones, he replied 'Only one'. He showed Barry a convict from Robben Island, Jan Kiser, who had one leg fractured and the other surrounded by a heavy chain. The climax came when Dr Barry ordered a mentally deranged man to be treated in hospital and not simply thrown into the asylum. Barry stated that the man's state might be 'the result of bad treatment he had received in the jail'. This criticism really upset the applecart.

Barry was summoned to give evidence on 15 September 1825. He refused to take the oath or to answer questions and was ordered to be imprisoned for one month for contempt of court. The Governor then intervened and overruled the sentence. Barry remained stubbornly persistent in his criticism of conditions. On 12 January 1826 he resigned all his official appointments. Public esteem for him was high but the administrative officials hated him. To settle what was becoming an awkward situation,

Opposite The Jonkershuis was originally built as the home of the landowner's eldest son.

he was promoted to staff surgeon and in 1828 transferred to Mauritius.

Promotions and transfers followed in steady succession, the West Indies, St Helena, Malta, deputy inspector of hospitals stationed at Corfu, and in 1858 to one of the highest medical ranks in the British Army, inspector-general stationed in Canada. There his health broke down. He was used to living in warmer climates. Bronchitis and influenza forced him to retire in 1859. He returned to London and died on 15 July 1865. Rumours about the sex of Dr Barry had intrigued so many people that the military authorities ordered an examination of the corpse. The person who laid out the body stated that Barry was a woman and, moreover, had given birth. To finally settle the mystery, the army surgeons reported to the registrar-general of Somerset House that Dr Barry was 'neither male nor female, but rather an imperfectly developed man'. There was no evidence to support the story that as a woman she had given birth. Dr Barry, she or he, died still an enigma.

The Cloetes were a fruitful family. One of them, Dirk, acquired Alphen in 1850. The house was already well furnished but to it the new owners took many of their own treasures, including a magnificent 17th century kist which had contained the family effects from Europe when they sailed with Van Riebeeck. They settled in and Dirk began planting vines. One of his sons, Louis, was sent to France to study wine-making. On his return he built the great cellar, renovated the manor-house, and started making wine.

The oldest son, Henry, inherited the estate but he was an advocate in Johannesburg and he left the running of Alphen to his younger brother, Louis. In the difficult political period leading to the Anglo-Boer war, Henry was pro-British. He served as British agent in Pretoria when the British diplomatic mission was withdrawn. When the war was imminent, Henry returned to stay in Alphen until peace came. With him came his wife Christina Deliana, daughter of Nicholaas van Warmelo who had brought the Nederduitse Hervormde Kerk to South Africa from Holland. She was very pro-Boer in the conflict and, unknown to her husband, set up a spy network based on Alphen. It was an excellent base, a great resort of high-ranking British officers such as Lord Kitchener and Lord Roberts. She found eavesdropping on their after-dinner conversations particularly informative. This information she placed in a hollow oak on the farm, where it was collected by undercover couriers and conveyed to Pretoria concealed in cases with false bottoms and hand-made dolls with hollow porcelain heads.

Apart from her espionage work, Mrs Cloete performed her wifely duties. She had four daughters and then at last came the longed-for son. Henry threw a great dinner to celebrate the birth of his heir. At the height of proceedings the nurse rushed in asking for a little brandy for the baby. There were roars of laughter from the guests and comments about a young chip off the old block. The next morning, however, the baby was dead, and a period of gloom settled on the house.

THE BERGVLIET ESTATE

Groot Constantia, with its manor-house, cellars and vineyards, is the classic wine estate of the Cape. It is hospitable and proud to display its treasures to visitors. It is a provider of good food and fresh grapes, especially of the muscatel varieties, picked and sold from February to June. Wine of course is available throughout the year, in several varieties and vintages, its cellars open for inspection and the sale of their contents direct to the public. If no other of the great wine estates in the Cape are visited, Groot Constantia must not be missed. It is a unique part of the history of the people of South Africa.

Several other parts of the fragmented original Groot Constantia estate of Simon van der Stel are also open to visitors. A tour through the Constantia Wine Route, as it is known, is very rewarding, full of beguiling scenes and interest. Start this journey from the entrance to the Groot Constantia estate on the main Constantia-Hout Bay road. A kilometre down this road, just before it reaches the Constantia Village centre, turn right at a traffic light into an oak-shaded street known as Ladies Mile and Ladies Mile Extension. Follow this road for one kilometre until it reaches another traffic light where it crosses the road named after the Spaanschemat ('Spanish rushes') River.

The Ladies Mile road leads over the Simon van der Stel freeway and then continues for 2 km until it ends by joining the lower main road. The Ladies Mile passes through a completely built-up area. In 1714 this was one of the three divisions of Groot Constantia sold at auction. One of the sections was Bergvliet ('Mountain stream').

When the British occupied the Cape in 1795, they found Bergvliet, then owned by Hendrik Oostwald Eksteen, to be in a very prosperous condition. Eksteen, however, was a supporter of current French revolutionary ideals. This made him very suspect by the conservative British, who regarded ideas of liberty, equality and fraternity as akin to the pox. Thus, when Eksteen sent out invitations to his daughter's wedding at Bergvliet and addressed them to Citizen so-and-so, Lord Macartney sent a party of rough-and-ready dragoons to arrive on the scene at the height of festivities, shoulder their way to the food and devour it with the manners of a pride of lions. The practice of 'quartering' dragoons on persons of known sympathies to revolutionary ideals became common. Feeding and accommodating such rowdy men subdued many farmhouses in the Cape, with young women sent far away for safety.

A climax came in the story of Bergvliet when the wealthy widow, Leanora Colyn of De Hoop op Constantia, built a house, as a present for one of her sons, on a portion of the original Bergvliet which she had purchased. She called it Sweet Valley. This farm lay on the south side of Bergvliet and was reached by a rough farm road crossing part of Bergvliet. When the Colyn family had bought De Hoop op Constantia, the original deed of sale dividing the property from Bergvliet gave the owners of De Hoop op Constantia rights in perpetuity to the use of this and other roads.

Hendrik Oostwald Eksteen didn't like the widow Colyn and she didn't care a fig for him. They disagreed in politics and practically everything else. She deliberately made full and flamboyant use of her right of way on the road across Bergvliet, galloping backwards and forwards each day to see her son, and sending wagons and carts to convey building materials for the new house and bring back thatching material for her own home. Eksteen seethed with rage. One day he put his slaves to work digging a deep ditch directly across the road. Leonora Colyn promptly appealed to the court and judgement was against Eksteen.

Thus began the so-called 'battle of Constantia'. It was a lawyer's delight, two wealthy people determined to fight each other to the bitter end no matter the cost. Advocates were briefed. The judge tried to arrange an out-of-court settlement but the contestants were adamant. Advocate Olof Bergh, for Eksteen, pleaded that the deed of sale gave the widow rights to use the paths and roads of Bergvliet but not to go across it. Advocate Johannes Truter, for Leonora Colyn, responded that Eksteen, in personal pique, was simply trying to deny a right which had been enjoyed without argument for a hundred years.

Eksteen won the case. The widow appealed to the King in Council, the first time this had been done by a resident of the Cape. In 1827 His Majesty ruled in favour of Leonora Colyn. 'Ladies Mile', the road which runs through Bergvliet, was thenceforth named after this celebrated and costly squabble. It proved to be the ruination of Eksteen. Costs were awarded against him. They were murderous and he went insolvent.

So far as Leonora, the redoubtable lady of the Ladies Mile was concerned, she died in 1839. Her son, Johannes Nicolaas, inherited De Hoop op Constantia. Eventually, the Board of Management of Groot Constantia bought the manor-house and the remaining thirteen hectares of ground; the rest of De Hoop op Constantia estate is lost under housing development. But at least a little was saved.

KLEIN CONSTANTIA

To discover the fate of the other portions of the original Constantia estate, let us go back to the crossroads where Ladies Mile extension crosses the Spaanschemat River road. From this point, instead of continuing straight, turn right down this road. After another kilometre the road diverges left

Opposite Although closely pressed by suburbia, Constantia retains its rural atmosphere.

slightly, while the Klein Constantia road branches off diagonally on the right. For an all-too-short 3 km this road leads through trees and past gardens of flowers. The estate known as De Hoop op Constantia lies on the right with a glimpse of its lovely manor-house peeping through the trees. Passing a turn-off to the left leading to the estate of Buitenverwachting, the road enters the grounds of Klein Constantia.

Klein Constantia was part of Simon van der Stel's original Groot Constantia. When Hendrik Cloete acquired the estate in 1772 and set out to revive its sagging agricultural industry, he soon discovered that some of the best wine-producing grapes flourished on this portion of Constantia and on the adjoining portion of De Hoop op Constantia. Both areas came under considerable cultivation of the grape varieties, Pontac and Muscat de Frontinac, used in the production of the famous red and white Constantia wines. There was no manor-house on Klein Constantia then, but on a particularly pleasant site, Cloete planted a grove of oak trees close to a mountain stream which was directed to feed a dam. A secluded guest-house was built in this pleasant area and named Marlbrook, the popular name of the renowned British general, the Duke of Marlborough, whose powerful support put on the throne of England, William of Orange, defender of the Protestant faith. Both men were much admired by Hendrik Cloete. The death of Hendrik brought a decline in the fortune of Groot Constantia from the golden years of the famed Constantia wines. His widow, Anna Catharina, had the task of controlling what seemed like a Cloete tribe of children and grandchildren.

Anna Catherina was a tough matriarch who seemed to revel in incessant family feuds. One of her sons, Johan Gerhard, in 1819, bought the 195 ha portion of the old estate known as Klein Constantia. He built the manor-house but failed to achieve notable success in farming. Thereafter Klein Constantia declined under a succession of owners. Some tried their best, but for so beautiful a place there seemed to be a blight. The Van der Byl family had it from 1890 to 1909. During this period the pioneer fruit nurseryman, Harry Pickstone, rented Marlbrook and planted there experimental orchards of fruit and beds of strawberries.

In 1913, however, Klein Constantia was acquired by a couple who at least gave it some renown in the social life of the Cape. The couple were Mr and Mrs Abraham Lochner de Villiers. He had been a milliner in Paarl and was nicknamed 'La Mode' from the name of his shop. He saved enough money from his business to take a holiday in Europe. Before departing he jocularly told his friends that he intended marrying a millionairess. He did. Clara Hussey, whose money came from the Pittsburgh steel mills, was the lady.

Back in the Cape the millinery shop was soon sold. Clara purchased Klein Constantia and, with her husband, set out to convert the somewhat run-down manor-house into a romantic scene of parties, balls, banquets, fun and games and all manner of social occasions. Some farming was also undertaken, but not much.

Clara made spacious additions to the manor-house, including a chapel, a ballroom with a gallery for an orchestra and a swimming-pool renowned for what the servants discreetly described as 'moonlight frolics'. Clara often had 600 guests at her all-night parties, sometimes inviting all the passengers and officers of passing cruise-liners to join in a grand jollification. A ghostly whisper of giggling and the popping of champagne corks is still said to be heard from the pool on some warm summer nights. The couple had no children. Lochner died in 1930 aged 61. Clara was four years older than him but she lived to the ripe age of 90 before dying in 1955. Jan de Villiers, nephew of Lochner, inherited the estate but he had insufficient finance to run the place.

In 1980 Douglas Jooste, after the merger of his family-owned company, Sedgwick Tayler, with Stellenbosch Farmers' Winery, bought Klein Constantia. He set out to revive its capability of producing fine wines. One of his dreams was to recreate at least one of the two legendary Constantia wines of the days of Hendrik Cloete. Supported by the advice of Professor Chris Orffes, the authority on wine varieties, the viticulturist Ernst le Roux, the master wine-maker Ross Gower, and his own enthusiastic son Lowell, he began a ten-year period of experimentation.

All that was certain was that some unspecified areas of the estate had produced the grapes needed in producing the two Constantia wines, Muscat de Frontinac for the white and Pontac for the red wine.

Both these cultivars had fallen out of favour in Cape viticulture but some relics of the original vines were found still growing where Van der Stel or Cloete had planted them. These were cloned and a vineyard planted with Muscat de Frontinac vines. The steppe buzzards then obliged by doing their job as guardians. The ripening grapes were selectively pruned and the remaining berries were left to a slow ripening until they had the appearance almost of shrivelled raisins with a taste like honey gathered by bees from the wild flowers and aromatic shrubs of the Cape. The first harvest was picked and crushed in 1986 and the young wine put into wood for a leisurely period of reflection and maturation. To the winemakers this was the most difficult part of the operation, as Ross Gower said, 'waiting for it, just waiting for it'.

In 1989 the first bottle was opened and they tasted it. Was it exactly the same as the famed Constantia white wine of the past days? It is impossible to know. Taste it yourself. Vin de Constance, as it is named, has a luscious sweetness, a lingering fragrance of the Cape mountains, a taste which could only come from a combination of the soils, winds and lush vegetation of the floral kingdom of the Cape. The great experiment has now started with a vineyard planted with Pontac grapes. The objective is a red Vin de Constance.

BUITENVERWACHTING

The neighbouring estate to Klein Constantia is Buitenverwachting ('Beyond expectations'), reached by a turn-off from the Klein Constantia road a little less than a kilometre before it enters the Klein Constantia estate. From this turn-off it is another kilometre to the manor-house, cellars and restaurant.

The estate with its werf (farmyard) in a magnificent garden setting has had, for so lovely a place, a curious history of disappointment. Originally the area was part of the estate of Bergvliet, itself a portion of Groot Constantia. In 1793 Hendrik Oostwald Eksteen, owner of Bergvliet, sold 200 morgen of the estate to Cornelis Brink, who sold most of it to his brother Arend in 1794.

Arend Brink gave his estate its name in 1796 and built the manor-house. He planted vines and had high hopes of fortune, but beauty is sometimes treacherous. A cheque-book farmer can only last as long as his bank balance. In 1797 Brink sold the farm to Ryk Arnoldus Mauritius Cloete, a brother of Hendrik Cloete of Groot Constantia. Ryk was a lot different from Hendrik. His farming industry seemed to consist principally of borrowing money and speculating in slaves. He bought, sold, long-term leased and short-term hired human beings. He lived too well on the proceeds. Ryk Cloete went bankrupt. He moved to the family refuge of Marlbrook and left the mess to a liquidator to handle. The whole property and all its chattels was auctioned off and sold to another Cloete (Pieter Lourens). Of the roster of slaves it is interesting to see that their value ranged around 350 rixdollars for a skilled worker. The lowest was 6 rixdollars for a three-year-old boy who was bought by a free maid, Betjie by name, who bid from the crowd and, it is hoped, had the sympathy of the assembly who failed to run up the price, realising that the woman had so little to her name and wanted to possess what was apparently her son.

Over the following years seventeen successive owners attempted to farm the estate with little success and several bankruptcies. One of the owners, the abovementioned Pieter Lourens Cloete, went so far as to change the name of the estate to Plumstead in the hope that this would bring better luck. It didn't, not to him.

In 1981, Richard Müller bought the estate and launched a comprehensive plan to realise, at last, its potential as a producer of fine wine. In the midst of a considerable investment in capital and creativity, the new owner, however, found himself in an awkward position. It was the time of the so-called 'Cold War'. Richard Müller was accused of complicity in supplying the Soviet Union with high-tech computers. He found it expedient to leave South Africa and make his home in East Europe, continuing his proj-

Opposite Buitenverwachting came close to destruction before being restored to its original gabled splendour

ects on Buitenverwachting through a management trust. The work continued with complex three-directional ploughing. The clay and the top soils were mixed to a depth of one metre. This ensured that moisture be maintained in the soil and provided the depth necessary for root development. It was the intention that natural rainfall would be the sole source of moisture. Organic farming techniques were introduced with no artificial fertilisers, herbicides or pesticides.

In May 1989, Richard Müller's wife, Sieglinde, took over the estate from the trust and ambitious development continued under her direct management. Today the modern state-of-the-art cellar produces a range of fine wines. Visitors are welcome. There are tours, tastings and direct sale of wine to visitors during normal business hours. A considerable dairy industry is also maintained on the estate, and there is a restaurant of high repute. It is interesting to see that a small block of hanepoot table grapes, about 100 years old, has been left in the midst of the modern cultivars and still rewards the owner for continued life by yielding great bunches of delicious grapes.

UITSIG AND TOKAI

To the right of the Spaanschemat River is a cricket oval complete with a Victorian pavilion – a surprising sight in so intense an agricultural setting. Constantia Uitsig ('Constantia view') is the delight of David McCay, a Johannesburg banker with a passion for cricket, wine, and Constantia. When he bought the property in 1988, together with a 60 ha portion of neighbouring Nova Constantia, it was little more than a neglected vineyard, a broken-down old cellar and a forlorn atmosphere – a little lost dog of a place, waiting to be put down by some real-estate speculator. The assets were a panoramic view and a rambling Victorian farmhouse in a lovely garden shaded by trees.

The new owner, supported by an enthusiastic staff, set to work to reinvigorate the estate. A comprehensive planting of new vines transformed the vineyards. Constantia Uitsig may be the smallest of the wine farms but the resolve was to make it one of the best. From past years, only the wonderful old hanepoot dessert grapes were left untouched and each season they are still sold from a stall beside the Spaanschemat road. The farmhouse has been converted into a restaurant featuring traditional Cape cuisine with vegetables, herbs, salads and artichokes grown on the estate, and is rated among the most popular restaurants of South Africa. Twelve luxurious guest cottages have also been built in the shady garden.

Beyond the entrance to Constantia Uitsig, the Spaanschemat River road continues southwards. After one kilometre it enters the area of the estate named Tokai, after the hills in Hungary where the decorative, subtly flavoured Tokai grapes had their original home and still produce a famous wine. In 1792 a German mercenary soldier, Johan Andreas Rauch, bought

the land but sold it in the same year to another German soldier, Andreas Georg Teubes, who in 1796 built the manor-house, designed for him by that indefatigable architect Louis Thibault. The house was a picture but within twelve months Herr Teubes put it up for auction, along with 70 000 growing vines, wagons, bullocks, wine caskets empty and full, good slaves and furniture of different kinds.

Johan Caspar Loos, a deacon to the German Lutheran community, became the next owner and he kept it until 1814. Then it was bought by Petrus Michiel Eksteen, son of the litigious Hendrik Oostwald Eksteen of Bergvliet. Wild times came to Tokai. Eksteen was a high roller, a rake and a profligate seemingly determined to ruin himself and his family. He wined, dined and lived on borrowed money and time. His wife was a Cloete, his sister the mistress of Alphen. In the beginning his credit was good. The parties he threw in the manor-house were famous. At one of them, on a New Year's eve, a celebrated ghost story of the Cape had its origin.

A vainglorious young man, said by some to have been one of the numerous Eksteens, accepted a bet on a boast he had made that he could ride his horse up the steps, into the dining-room, around the table and then down the steps again. Egged on by his friends the young man called for his horse to be saddled, rode up the steps into the dining-room, around the table, had a drink of brandy from the saddle, poured a good tot into the horse's mouth and then, to loud applause and cheers, galloped off out of the room, across the stoep and took off over the high flight of curving steps. Horse and rider were killed. The ghosts of the two are said to come galloping out of the surrounding trees each New Year's eve and repeat the performance.

Above Constantia Uitsig (Constantia view) has so-called 'holbol' (concavo-convex) end gables.

Petrus Michiel Eksteen went bankrupt, and eventually, in 1883, the Tokai estate was bought by the Cape government and given to the Forestry Department. Joseph Storr Lister, the man regarded as the pioneer of forestry in Southern Africa, moved into the manor-house with his wife Georgina and created the foundation forestry nursery for the government policy of reforestation in the Cape and later throughout South Africa. Lister was appointed as the first Superintendent of Woods and Forests. His salary was £10 a month for himself and £5 for his horse. Both were granted free accommodation in the Tokai manor-house and stables.

Lister had learned the art and science of forestry in India, where he had gone after completing schooling in Cape Town. At Tokai he planted an arboretum of trees, collected from many parts of the world, in his search for those species most suited to South Africa, a country where timber trees, especially quick-growing soft-woods, were in short supply. He cultivated great numbers of pine and eucalyptus on the slopes of Prinseskasteel (Constantiaberg); the lower areas he devoted to American vine cuttings, which were resistant to phylloxera, and which he supplied to the Cape wine estates to revive the vineyards destroyed by the disease.

It was all a lot of work, but to Joseph Lister a labour of love. His dedication to the lovely world of trees and plants drew, perhaps, a little inspiration from the knowledge that Robert Brown, the Scottish botanical scientist so famous in later years, had walked the same good Tokai earth decades before. Brown's ship, on its way to Australia, called in at Simon's Bay in October 1802. Brown and his party wanted exercise and the chance to see something of the Cape. They set out to walk to Cape Town. Caught by a rainstorm and lost, they arrived at Tokai. The owner, then, was Johan Loos. He was away in Cape Town but a pleasant young lady received them graciously, fed them and persuaded them to stay the night, bedded snug on feather mattresses while the rain pelted down all night on the thatched roof. The next morning they walked on, climbed Table Mountain and then, with a load of botanical specimens, walked back to Tokai.

Forester Lister, after only three years' happy stay in Tokai, was transferred to King William's Town and eventually took charge of the Cape Province's forestry department. The plantation he created at Tokai flourished and today is the setting of a school of forestry. The reserve provides pleasant walking, riding and picnicking for the public. It is open daily from dawn to dusk.

STEENBERG

The Spaanschemat River road, changing its name to Orpen Road, leads through the Tokai forest for 2 km and then crosses the Tokai main road

Opposite Tokai and the farmlands of Constantia valley, seen from Ou Kaapse Weg.

and eventually, after a right turn, and after changing its name to Steenberg Road, continues southwards with the great estate of Steenberg ('Stone mountain') on the right and the sombre Pollsmoor Prison on the left. The prison was built on the site of a former Grand Prix motor-racing track created just before the Second World War on the farm owned in the 1870s by Hendrik van der Poll and his wife Johanna Kirsten, after whose family Kirstenbosch is named. After 2 km the Steenberg road passes the entrance to the Steenberg estate, with the manor-house and original farm building still standing in superb condition.

Steenberg originally had the name Swaaneweide ('Feeding place of swans'). Its first owner was an extraordinary young woman named Catharina Ustings who arrived in the Cape in 1662, a 22-year-old widow from Lübeck on the Baltic coast of Germany. What her short history had been it would be interesting to know. She survived the appalling conditions of a sea voyage from Europe to the Cape, landed just ten years after Jan van Riebeeck's founding of the Tavern of the Sea, and considered it wise to get herself safely married as soon as possible. A young, single woman could experience rather rough handling in those times and parts. Her choice of husband was Hans Ras. He was a former soldier who had become a free burgher settled in the valley of the Liesbeek River on property he had acquired from Jacob Cloete.

The marriage started with an uproarious wedding day. On the way home from the church the two wagons conveying guests and the married couple were raced against each other by highly intoxicated drivers. There was a collision. The incensed bridegroom received a knife between his ribs while he was involved in a brawl with the drivers. His wife pulled the knife out of her husband and managed to get him home but there was little joy in the marriage night.

Hans Ras survived the knife wound and had time to father several children before he was killed by a lion. Catharina married again but the new husband was murdered by one of the locals. Catharina tried again but husband number three was trampled to death by an elephant. Catharina was persistent. A woman on her own faced many hazards in those days. She selected Matthys Michelse as number four. By that time she had also reputedly become the part-time mistress of Simon van der Stel. She persuaded the Governor to grant her the farm she named Swaaneweide. Van der Stel was pleased to oblige. In 1682 Catherina and her husband built their first house on this farm. By the time Simon van der Stel retired to his estate of Groot Constantia, Catherina was well established and a personality of some renown in the Cape. When the commissioner, Baron van Rheede tot Drakenstein, rode on inspection through the lowlands below the Steenberge, he and his party lunched with her, finding the food excellent but having some views about the lady. 'She rides bare-back like an Indian,' the baron wrote, 'and her children resemble Brazilian cannibals.'

In 1695 Catharina sold the farm to Frederick Russouw and moved to the valley of the Berg River. Russouw's wife, Christina Diemer, was a woman in the same resolute mould as Catharina. While her husband farmed, she provided a continuity of effective management which saw the farm develop, especially after 1741 when the horrific wrecks in Table Bay induced the Dutch East India Company to make Simon's Bay a winter refuge for shipping. She became the principal supplier of provisions for ships anchoring off Simon's Town. She also acquired the grant of additional land from Baron von Imhoff, Governor-General of the Netherlands East Indies, including what she named Imhoff's Gift, the site of the modern village of Kommetjie. She and a gentleman friend, Carol Georg Wieser, a wealthy farmer, built two seaside cottages at what was destined to become a popular resort next to the natural tidal pool, the kommetjie ('Little basin') which gave the place its name.

Over the decades the estate changed hands two or three times, but there was continuity – it remained more or less within the family – and it was generally well managed. It prospered. Finally, in 1990, it was sold to the Johannesburg Consolidated Investment Company, Limited (JCI). Under this ownership a vast transformation has come to Steenberg. The lower-lying portion, with soil of less agricultural potential, has been converted into an 18-hole golf-course directly fronted by 210 residential erven as homes for wealthy golf-lovers. The design of the central clubhouse is harmonious with the historic architecture of the estate. A state-of-the-art wine cellar is surrounded by new vineyards with cultivars selected to suit the chemical nature of the soils, micro-climate and altitude of the slopes of the Steenberge.

DEATH OF A PRINCESS

The wine estates of Constantia all lie with their backs resting against the narrow spinal range of sandstone mountains which run southwards from Table Mountain down the Peninsula to its tip at Cape Point, where the Cape of Good Hope provides the south-western end to the continent of Africa. A number of springs have their source on these mountains. Of some of these there is a curious legend concerning the final decline of the pastoral tribes who had once grazed their herds and flocks in the area of the Cape Peninsula and the Hottentots Holland.

After the 'purchase' by the Dutch East India Company in 1672 of the Cape Peninsula, the Hottentots Holland and most of the interior as far as what were called the Mountains of Africa, the once dominant tribes, who had themselves supplanted the earlier inhabitants, and now been themselves swindled out of the area, fell to petty squabbling and dissipating their remaining wealth in livestock by bartering for trinkets, scrap metal, alcohol and tobacco.

The Chainoukwa had been persuaded into selling their homeland of the Hottentots Holland to the Dutch East India Company for £6 16s 4d

worth of junk. The tribe had then fragmented under two contentious leaders, Prince Dorha (the original paramount chief known as Klaas to the Dutch) and a rival chieftain known as Koopman. Dorha was married to the daughter of Goukou, the ruler of the powerful and wealthy tribe of the Hessekwa, who lived in the area of the river known as the Riviersonderend ('River without end'). Goukou supported his son-in-law and, at first, so did the Dutch until there was a quarrel over cattle trading.

A punitive force of 100 soldiers and 100 burghers was sent from Cape Town to settle the matter. Koopman gleefully joined in the attack on his rival. Dorha and two of his leading men were arrested, and all their cattle were seized and shared among the attackers. Booty included the wife of Dorha, known as the Prinses ('Princess'). Dorha and his two companions were sent to Robben Island on 8 August 1683. Appeals on their behalf were made by several of the Dutch colonists who were friendly with Dorha, and by his father-in-law.

The authorities in Cape Town relented. Dorha and his companions were allowed to return to the mainland and settle near the site of modern Muizenberg. He begged for the return of his wife but the Prinses said she preferred to remain with Koopman. The two chiefs became mortal enemies. They both wanted the Prinses and to get her were prepared to ruin themselves and their people.

In the midst of this bloodshed, the Prinses changed her mind and ran away to rejoin her husband. Koopman pursued her. He claimed to have killed her but legend says that she feigned death and escaped to hide in the great cave known from its shape as the Elephant's Eye below the summit of the 928 m high Prinseskasteel ('Castle of the princess'), nowadays less romantically known as Constantiaberg.

In the cave the Prinses remained, hoping that the fighting would come to an end. Instead, in June 1701, Dorha was killed. Koopman was ruined and the Chainoukwa tribe dispersed. In her cave the Prinses is said to have wept bitterly at the death of her husband and the dissipation not only of the tribe but of her entire race. She committed suicide, and legend says that the springs on the mountain are forever reinforced with the magical sadness of her tears. They flow to the sea, replenishing on the way lakes which fill the hollows in the flat land below the mountains, Prinsesvlei ('Princess marsh'), Klein Prinsesvlei ('Little princess marsh'), Zandvlei ('Sandy marsh'), Rondevlei ('Round marsh;) and Zeekoevlei ('Hippopotamus marsh'). These lakes today provide recreation for the people of the Cape Peninsula. Perhaps the tears still shed today by the sad Prinses are as much for the degeneration of her lakes through pollution as for the dissipation of her people.

Above Silvermine – these alien pines have since been felled and fynbos, in the foreground, now flourishes throughout.

CHAPTER FIVE

THE SOUTHERN PENINSULA

THE MAIN DUAL CARRIAGEWAY ROAD known as Paradise Road, after passing the turn-off to Claremont, takes on the name of Edinburgh Drive and eventually climbs the slopes of what Van Riebeeck named the Wynberg ('Wine mountain'). As it tops the rise, there is a fine view over the Cape Flats and towards False Bay, with a first glimpse in the distance of the tip of the Cape Peninsula, which is the principal objective of this pleasant journey.

On the summit of the hill, 12 km from city centre, there is a turn-off left past the stone pines, oaks and silver trees of Wynberg Park. By turning left here and again after passing the second traffic-light, the traveller enters the suburb of Wynberg.

FROM WYNBERG TO THE OLD CAPE WAY

Wynberg is a substantial and very congested commercial centre, but it does have its charming side – many of its old cottages have been restored in what is locally known as 'Chelsea' style. In these a community of artists, craftspeople and would-be artists have made their homes and studios. The park and the open-air theatre of Maynardville are also in the Chelsea area of Wynberg.

James Maynard, after whom the park is named, was a 19th-century timber merchant and member of the Cape Legislative Assembly. His daughter's son, William Maynard Farmer, who inherited the estate in 1874, accumulated wealth in the exciting days of the diamond rushes, lived in style and created a colourful ornamental garden of oleanders, hydrangeas, fountains and lawns (his gardener was trained at London's Kew). In due course the property came under municipal control to become a park and an open-air theatre, venue of an annual summer Shakespeare production in an idyllic setting. The original homestead has been demolished, but several ghosts of its grand days reputedly linger on. These include a cast-off, unwed daughter with babe in arms and rapidly receding horse's hooves, said to be either the culprit fleeing or the father in pursuit.

Right Boat trips to Seal Island are run from Kalk Bay harbour. The island also attracts numerous sharks.

Mining magnates also raised mansions in Wynberg. The controversial Sir Joseph ('J.B.') Robinson built Hawthornden in the style of a French country house, with elegant balconies and cast iron, including a greenhouse to supply his kitchen with fresh vegtables. Also in Herschel Walk is Trovato, a stone-built mansion described as being in the 'millionaire institutional tradition' and erected as the Cape home of Carl Jeppe to the design of Sir Herbert Baker.

Back to the double carriageway, which continues southwards across an undulating, green and pleasant landscape. There are turn-offs to suburbs such as Diep River, Bergvliet and Meadowridge. At 20 km from the city, a road to the left leads to the suburb of Retreat and, on the right, to the forest area of Tokai. Retreat was always closely connected with the British army, which established two camps there – Pollsmoor and Westlake, both used as marshalling and resting-places for troops in transit to Asia or Europe, especially during the two world wars. With the interminable movement of manpower during those years, countless numbers of men

found themselves quartered in Retreat, and it remains an address remembered by many.

From the turn-off to Retreat and Tokai, the Simon van der Stel freeway continues for 1,5 km and then reaches an intersection. To the left are Lakeside and Muizenberg, to the right the scenic Ou Kaapse Weg (old Cape way), a superb drive that begins with a steady climb up the Steenberg ('Stony mountain'), reaching a grand viewsite on the summit. A turn-off leads to a parking area and, further on, to a toll-gate providing entry into a magical land of pine forests and picnic sites. The whole area is known as the Silvermine Nature Reserve, now part of the Cape Peninsula National Park, and it is rich in indigenous flora. Even the verges of the road are gardens of wild flowers, brilliant with colour, especially in spring. Pause awhile at the viewsite and look down at the tidal wave of housing relentlessly pressing the fertile farmlands of Constantia back against the stony mountains. You can almost see, and certainly sense, the dynamics of this movement, of humanity trampling to oblivion the good earth which sustains them.

There are many pleasant picnic places in the nature reserve and the walks are delightful. One of them takes you to the great cave of the Elephant's Eye with its memories of the sad princess (see page 74). Notable, too, is the circular route up the forest road which leads from the reservoir to the summit of the mountain and then down to the other side of the reservoir. Near the highest point of the road, a short walk away, the stone beacon on top of Noordhoek Peak (756 m above sea-level) may be seen. From this beacon there is a spectacular view of Hout Bay and the sea, surrounded by beach and mountain.

One kilometre further along the Ou Kaapse Weg, beyond the turn-off to the summit viewsite and toll-gate, there is another digression, this one on the left-hand side of the road. A gate, open during daylight hours, allows access to another popular picnic area close to a waterfall which, in the wet winter months, presents an attractive spectacle. From here there are walks to the Kalk Bay and Muizenberg mountains with their caves,

Opposite From sheltered Table Bay, the Peninsula extends south to far distant Cape Point.

some perhaps still to be discovered, wild flowers and glorious views over False Bay.

At the turn-off to the Ou Kaapse Weg, the main double carriageway of the Simon van der Stel freeway comes to an end. Turn left (the right turn, as we've noted, takes you to the Silvermine reserve) and in due course you're in the seaside suburb of Muizenberg, 26 km from city centre.

FALSE BAY

The coastal road is narrow and congested, especially on holidays and sunny weekends when half of the population of Cape Town seems to be travelling along it to reach their chosen recreational areas on the False Bay coast. Muizenberg is justly ranked as one of the world's more famous seaside resorts. The glory of the place is its beach, the finest and most spacious on the coast of Southern Africa. The offshore waters are warm, and safe for bathing.

Above A black-headed heron finds abundant food in the shallows. The Cape Flats lakes are a haven for bird-life.

The town lies on the northwestern end of False Bay, a 30 km by 30 km inlet of the sea held between the mountainous arms of the Cape Peninsula. During the summer months, when the prevailing wind is the powerful southeaster, the warm Mozambique-Agulhas Current from the Indian Ocean flows down as far as the Cape of Good Hope. False Bay lies at the end of its journey down the east coast. The bay fills with sparkling blue water, warmed to about 22°C and well populated with Indo-Pacific species of fish. This is in the summer-holiday time – False Bay is at its best from November to April. The splendid beach stretches east to west for 35 unbroken kilometres. Rudyard Kipling, who knew and loved the place, was a regular summer visitor, swam with his friend Cecil Rhodes in the azure water, strolled bare-foot along the beach and, in 1895, wrote his poem 'The Flowers', which contains the oft-quoted line 'White as the sands of Muizenberg, spun before the gale'. Rhodes, whose lungs were weakened by years of tuberculosis, bought (in 1899) a seaside cottage beside the coastal road and spent as much time as he could in this unpretentious little place, and the fresh air he loved to breathe in long, deep breaths seemed to be his last links to his fragile life.

The magnificent beach stretches off eastwards to the mountain range of the Hottentots Holland. Baden-Powell Drive follows the shoreline, providing an attractive panorama of glistening sands and restless surf. There are kilometres of safe and enjoyable bathing, surfing and fishing stretches, such as those at Strandfontein; Mnandi and Swartklip, 18 km from Muizenberg. From Swartklip the road veers inland to join Settlers Way.

Strandfontein has been developed as a recreational area for suburbs such as Mitchell's Plain, and has a large tidal pool, caravan park, some bungalows and wind-protected picnic grounds, as well as the Strandfontein Snake, Crocodile and Reptile Park.

At Mnandi there is a large pool with slides and boat rides; at Swartklip a resort known as Monwabisi (which means 'The one which makes others happy') with the largest tidal pool in the southern hemisphere plus picnic spots, camping and caravanning grounds and shops. Swartklip has been developed, particularly, as a resort for the residential area named Khayelitsha ('New home').

Close to the shores of False Bay lie several lakes, fed by streams which have sources mainly in the mountains of Constantia and Tokai. On reaching the level ground of the Cape Flats, these streams half lose themselves in the sandy former sea bed in depressions which trap their flow and become shallow lakelets such as Sandvlei ('Sandy marsh'), beloved by canoeists, owners of small yachts, windsurfers and by numerous birds. Around Sandvlei's shores is Marina da Gama, an extensive luxury housing project with waterside sites opening on to a series of artificial canals – an imaginative residential concept, built on what was originally a garbage dump and wasteland.

The Diep River supplies water from the two connected lakelets known as Little Princess Vlei and Big Princess Vlei, valued for the size of the carp living in their waters. Two other lakelets fed by water from the mountains and from other sources are Zeekoeivlei ('Hippopotamus marsh'), the largest of them all and a favourite haunt of yachtsmen, and Rondevlei ('Round marsh'), a famous bird sanctuary established in 1952 as the first ornithological field station in South Africa. In this 105 ha sanctuary some 200 bird species make their home or are occasional visitors, including flamingos and pelicans. The birds are systematically studied in relation to one another, to food and to climatic conditions, and are at their most prolific around midsummer. Visitors have access to observation towers and a hide, and to an interesting museum. Hippos were reintroduced to Rondevlei in 1981 in order to control the growth of vegetation.

Close to Rondevlei lie the extensive artificial lakes of the Strandfontein sewage disposal area. In these nutrient-rich waters live an array of water birds rivalling that of any of the world's famous bird sanctuaries. Flamingos (both the greater and lesser species), pelicans, avocets, stilts, innumerable ducks and other birds visit the area seasonally or live there permanently. Rondevlei is open to the public all year round.

False Bay, as the terminal of the Mozambique-Agulhas Current, is of great significance to marine biologists: there is constant seasonal change in the nature of its marine life. From April to June, for example, the rare and remarkable argonauts drift in, strange little creatures which have no powers of self-locomotion and are entirely at the mercy of wind, current and tide. Their exquisite, fragile shells, are easily damaged, especially those of the larger, more mature animals. If they are washed up in daylight the seabirds swoop on them, destroying the shells in order to feed on the animal inside. A large, undamaged argonaut shell is a valuable item – shells are sold to collectors and shops all over the world. To walk on the False Bay beach at night with a torch and to see an argonaut washed up unbroken at your feet is a real thrill, and rewards you with a real treasure.

The winter months in False Bay bring a profound change. The northwest wind replaces the summer southeaster. The warm Mozambique-Agulhas Current is pushed back with all its varied life-forms. The cold Benguela Current, a spin-off of the Antarctic Drift, flows into the bay. The water temperature drops to around 15°C. Cold-water species of marine life displace the warm-water species. Swimmers need to be of a hardier breed but surfers, protected in their wetsuits, find wave conditions to be far more exciting. The waves are larger, although the shallow water of the False Bay littoral acts as a brake – it slows them down, making the coast particularly safe for swimmers as well as novice surfers, who regard the area as their nursery. The

Opposite The suburb of Lakeside takes its name from the waters of Sandvlei.

only current in False Bay is a leisurely clockwise movement along the coast. Sharks, including the Great White, although present in the bay (as they are in all oceans), prefer deep water and, in any case, feed on the copious supply of seals who have their home on Seal Island in the middle of the bay.

STORY OF A TOWN

Muizenberg grew up as the principal recreational area for the Cape Peninsula, but its origins are more serious: it started life as a military stronghold intended to defend the narrow passage where the coastal road leads between the sea and the slopes of the mountain. The Oudepost (old post) building, erected there in 1743, still survives.

Imagine the place as it was in those days. To the south there stretched a rocky coast overlooked by towering cliffs. Only wild creatures such as baboons lived there and these were so numerous that the soldiers, we are told, dared not go out unless they were in parties of five or six. The post building looked eastwards over False Bay with it beach stretching away to the hotizon, at that period a place only of birds, of basking seals and the endless murmur of the surf.

Northwards, the post was linked to Cape Town by a sandy track, only 25 km long but, by its roughness, involving quite a difficult journey for the soldiers and their carts. Close to this road lay the shallow lake of Sandvlei, a place of pelicans, flamingos, coots, wild ducks and wonderful reflections from the water – of the dawns and sunsets and the distant shapes of Devil's Peak and Table Mountain. Wax-berries, milkwood trees and reeds grew around the lake while great shoals of baby fish found their way in from the sea via the estuary. The nutrient-rich waters of the lake acted as a nursery where the young fish could grow in safety until such time as instinct drew them to swim out once more into the open ocean.

The Muizenberg area has quite a dramatic place in the annals of the Cape. It was here that, in 1795, British troops led by Major-General J.H. Craig landed from a fleet of warships commanded by Admiral Sir George Elphinstone. This was the time of the French Revolutionary wars; the French had occupied the Netherlands, and the British, worried about the security of their vital sea-lane to the East, decided to pre-empt a possible invasion. There was some skirmishing around the outpost, the invaders were reinforced, and the Dutch forces (an infantry regiment plus artillery, mounted bughers and the 'coloured' Pandour Corps), led by Colonel Robert Gordon, a Dutchman of Scottish descent, retreated towards Cape Town, fighting a running battle that ended with the formal surrender of the Cape to the British.

Shortly afterwards Colonel Gordon committed suicide in the garden of his Cape Town home. It was said that he could not bear the jibe that the only time he had drawn his sword had been when he led his men out of the castle and commanded them to lay down their arms.

After the surrender there was perhaps an understandable tendency to celebrate amongst the British forces. The Cape Town taverns did a roaring trade.

Along the track from Muizenberg most of the farmhouses were looted, wine drunk, livestock stolen and some damage done. Even the grand manor-house of Groot Constantia, home of the renowned wine master, Hendrik Cloete, was visited by a stray party of roistering sailors who destroyed furniture, broke open several barrels of good wine and drank until they were incapable of any further activity. It is said that to make amends to the hospitable Mr Cloete, they later presented him with a collection of cannonballs fired during the battle of Muizenberg. These cannonballs may still be seen at Groot Constantia ornamenting the pillars of the lower vineyard.

In those days the track from Cape Town to Simon's Town was a long one for thirsty men. The few wayside farmhouses were not places of refreshment, and inns could only be established with profit when there was a steady demand by increased traffic along a better road. Such a state of affairs came about after the second British occupation of the Cape in 1806. Simon's Town in 1814 then became a Royal Navy base, and although the road from Cape Town still remained unmade it carried such a stream of travellers that wayside inns became viable.

One of the most celebrated of these inns was Merckel's Halfway House hotel, established by George Merckel at Diep River. After Merckel's death in 1839 his widow Hester married a renowned character of the Cape, Johan Georg Rathfelder, a big burly man who had been born in Stuttgart in 1811, emigrated to the Cape in 1835 and, through his marriage, became the host of what was renamed as Rathfelder's Halfway House. Dressed in black leather, shell jacket ornamented with chains, jackboots and helmet, riding a big bay horse, he maintained, at the hotel, the hounds of the Cape Hunt and, riding hard, he was almost the prototype in Southern Africa of the Hell's Angels. Known as the 'King of the Landlords', he kept an excellent table and good order in the establishment, with a clientele of Anglo-Indians on recuperative leave, enthusiasts of the hunt, passing sailors and many distinguished guests including Prince Alfred of England (in 1860). Rathfelder died in the hotel in 1873 and the building eventually became part of the former Eaton Convalescent Home.

Further along the road an equally famous wayside inn was established in Muizenberg in 1825 by two immigrants from Britain, the brothers Henry and Simon Peck. Farmer Peck's Inn, as it was called, was a rambling, thatched, white-walled building which stood on the site of the present town's tallest building, Cinnabar. A sign on the front showed the gentle shepherd of Salisbury Plain, a benevolent-looking rustic with a lamb under his arm. Above the sign was another board displaying an atrocious piece of verse, an effusion said to have been concocted by two midshipmen

who, unable to pay their bill after a night in the place, presented the hosts with the poem and painted the inn sign instead of paying cash. In the pub there was another sign which read:

This is a home for all those who haven't a home of their own, and a refuge for all who have one'.

The Pecks were reputed to be smugglers and purveyors of strong drink which had not known the revenue collector's seal of blessing. They were occasionally in trouble with the law but around their inn the seaside resort of Muizenberg had its start. Simon died in 1850 and Henry in 1857. Rathfelder from the Halfway House then bought the inn and it was run by his daughter, an enormously fat woman whose contented appearance was considered a considerable advertisement for the place. Apart from eating, she spent much of her time dozing in a double-sized rocking chair in a corner of the bar. Nothing remains of the building. The name Peck's Valley lingers on in a vale above Muizenberg.

MUIZENBERG TODAY

The village which developed around the inn started with a few fishermen's cottages, gradually attracted holidaymakers and became the rather atmospheric place of today. It is worth strolling through the narrow streets of what is known as the 'ghetto', and then, in Beach Road along 'Millionaires Row', the imposing line of mansions that were mostly built in Edwardian times as holiday homes for the wealthy of Johannesburg.

A magnificent feature of Beach Road are four adjoining houses designed by the celebrated architect, Herbert Baker. These houses – Crawford Lea, Rokeby, Sandhills and Swanbourne – became the possession of Joan St Leger Lindbergh, great granddaughter of Frederick St Leger, founder of the *Cape Times* newspaper and daughter of A.V. Lindbergh, a Rand financier and creator, amongst other enterprises, of the Central News Agency. His daughter was a poet and philanthropist. She consolidated the four houses and Swanbourne was opened on 28 August 1996 as the Joan St Leger Lindbergh Arts Foundation. In this handsome setting there are art exhibitions, lectures, readings and musical occasions. It is a fine cultural asset. There is a tea-room, reference library and conference facilities.

Muizenberg has a pavilion, swimming pools, miniature golf, children's playgrounds, a promenade, water slides and a pond for small motor boats. Trek fishermen still bring in hauls of harders (mullet), yellowtail, and other table fish. The beach stretches far away, inviting a swim, a paddle in the tidal zone, a night-time chance of finding an argonaut,

Opposite Majestic rollers advance in line, like disciplined battalions, upon 'the white sands of Muizenberg'.

tribute, dies disgraced', disbursed over £70 000 000 for the benefit of his fellow man. He died in 1919, aged 84.

The Carnegie Library building later became the police station, while the post office became the magistrate's court. The two eventually fell out of use but in June 1990 they were opened as the Police Museum, the first of its kind in the Western Cape. The various aspects of police life are depicted in displays of antique furniture and memorabilia of police duties in the field. In the office, there are photographs of old stations, chief magistrates, officials and detachments; historical snippets reflecting the development of the Cape police force prior to Union; and displays of uniforms and kits, arms and equipment. Also on view are authentic reconstructions of police single quarters, a police inspector's office of about 1948, a charge office, a periodical court-room, and police cells, complete with one prisoner trying to escape and another trying to set the building alight! The full gamut of the world of crime is well represented in the displays portraying notorious crimes of the past and of weapons used by criminals.

Next along the coastal road stands the elegant building named The Fort, built between 1929 and 1930 as the home of Count Natale Labia, who came to South Africa in 1916 as Italian Consul in Johannesburg and later his country's first minister plenipotentiary in South Africa. Count Labia married Ida, second daughter of the mining magnate, Sir J.B. Robinson. Their Muizenberg home was designed, on a grand scale, as the official residence of the Italian legation and became a renowned social and diplomatic centre with receptions, parties and the visits of innumerable celebrated people in the world of diplomacy and the arts. Count Labia died in 1936. The title of Prince was conferred upon him posthumously in recognition of distinguished service to his country. His wife, Princess Ida, died in 1961, and the house was leased as an embassy to the Canadian Government and then to the Argentinian Government. In 1983 it was presented by Prince Labia's son, Count Labia, with its treasures of art and design, to the people of South Africa, and is . now known as the Natale Labia Museum. The building, a national heritage site, was adapted for use as a museum and gallery in 1988. With its lecture rooms, gallery, restaurant and garden, it is an exquisite asset to the cultural life of the Cape.

Continuing down the Historic Mile, there are several interesting houses such as Canty Bay, Graceland, Knights, and Rust en Vrede, the mansion built in 1903 by the mining magnate Sir Abe Bailey. Graceland was the home of John Garlick, merchant prince and philanthropist. It is a superbly furnished and most elegant home in a garden which extends behind the house up the slopes of the mountains almost to the level of Boyes Drive. Paths take walkers through what is a sanctuary of wild flowers and beautiful trees.

Perhaps the most interesting of all the buildings of the Historical Mile is the small, almost insignificant, thatched Barkly Cottage, bought in 1899 by Cecil Rhodes as a seaside retreat with a small bedroom and a living-room.

The main coastal road continues its way southwestwards, passing the railway station built in 1913 to serve the suburban line opened in 1882. Several interesting and contrasting buildings line the right hand side of the road and provide what is known as the Historical Mile of Muizenberg. First after the railway station is the simple little building of De Post Huys ('The post house') which has been restored in modern times and is preserved as an historic monument. When the British occupied the Cape, the old building became the quarters of the commanding officer of the Muizenberg garrison, with three batteries, a powder magazine close to the sea, and a barracks on the site of the later Muizenberg park.

Just beyond De Post Huys stand two buildings. The first housed the original post office, erected on the site of the old toll house where all passing traffic had to stop and pay their dues for the use of the road. Next to this building stands the Carnegie Library, built in 1911 from a grant made by Andrew Carnegie, the great Scottish philanthropist who made a vast fortune in America, then returned to Scotland and, in accordance with his belief that 'a man who dies possessed of wealth which he was free to dis-

Above Colouful cubicles, locally known as 'bathing boxes', line the beach at St James.

It was there that Rhodes spent as much of his remaining life as he could, and there he died, on 26 March 1902. His close friends and associates were gathered to see him for the last time. From his deathbed he concluded the planning of and paperwork for the creation of the Rhodes Fruit Farms, destined to transform the entire fruit-growing and exporting industry of South Africa. He was only 49 years of age. It is said that his last words were 'So much to do, so little done'. His doctors could only despair – there was so much the matter with this man that it was only his indomitable will that had kept him alive so long. From birth he had suffered from a hole in the heart; His lungs were shattered by tuberculosis, and a drastic surgical procedure to arrest this wasting disease, which had travelled the length of his spinal column, left him, at the age of 17, a eunuch. He panted rather than breathed. The southeaster with its rush of pure, fresh air, actually seemed to sustain him in the last months of his life. A hole was knocked through the wall of his house to allow the wind to sweep in to his sickbed. Physically he was a wreck but he had achieved so much and left so much to Southern Africa and the world that his memory will long linger.

Rhodes Cottage, which is open to the public, is maintained with its original furniture and many interesting personal possessions and photographs concerned with the eventful life of a remarkable man.

THE KALK BAY AREA

On 5 October 1858 the foundation stone of a small church was laid to provide a place of worship for the Catholic community living along the coast between Muizenberg and Kalk Bay. A number of Filipino fishermen, survivors of a shipwreck, had settled in the area. They were Catholics and the nearest church to them was at Simon's Town. They supported the building of the new church. It was named in honour of the apostle and fisherman St James, who was also the patron saint of Spain. Spanish was the language of the Filipino fishermen. A priest rode from Wynberg each week to the church to say Mass.

On 1 June 1874, Father John Duignan, an Irish priest who could speak Spanish, was sent to serve the community. He was supposed to relieve only for six months but remained for 50 years. the St James Mission School was established close to the church, with Father Duignan and Francis Hilario as teachers to the children of the fisherfolk of Kalk Bay.

More people settled along the coast. The Cape Government Railways decided in 1900 that a proper station was needed to replace a simple whistle-stop, and they needed the site of the church for this station. John Duignan only assented on condition that the station be named St James. The indefatigable Duignan, supported by the Filipinos and other inhabitants of the coast, then set about building the handsome sandstone church of today. A larger school was also needed and this, with the aid of

Italian stonemasons, was also built of sandstone. The new convent school, named Star of the Sea, was opened at the beginning of 1908.

St James has a beach and tidal swimming pool sheltered from the southeast wind. An attractive residential area has made its appearance on the overlooking mountain slopes with grand views of False Bay. A walkway close to the sea links St James to Muizenberg 1,5 km away. Beyond St James the coastal road continues for a further 1,5 km and then, at the entrance to Kalk Bay harbour, joins the road coming down the slopes from the scenic sweep of Boyes Drive.

Kalk Bay ('Lime bay') takes its name from former years when kilns were burned to produce lime from shells for painting buildings. Quite a num-

Above left The view from Boyes Drive encompasses Kalk Bay and distant Simon's Town.

THE MOUNTAINS AND THEIR CAVES

Perhaps the area's most intriguing venues are the many remarkable caves, about which there is a story. In 1924 a schoolmaster by the name of Johannes Meyer spent a holiday at Kalk Bay, and on learning that there were caves in the mountains he followed the paths meandering up to the heights. His experiences entranced him so much that his holiday became a period of joyful discovery. The paths which made their way upwards, some steep and direct, others gradual and diagonal, rewarded him with memorable views. At his feet were gaily coloured wild flowers – heaths, proteas, everlastings, watsonias, scarlet-coloured flames and countless other lovely shrubs.

The caves added a touch of drama and adventure to this natural beauty. Several were already well known in the 1920s. Muizenberg Cave, with its enchanting moss-grown entrance, its low caverns and deep, mysterious well, had not yet been totally disfigured by morons with their idiotic name painting; but the process had started – the first graffito date was 1873. Clovelly Cave, with its labyrinth of passages and chambers, was sufficiently well known to be considered haunted by the local 'coloured' folk. Apparently a half-demented old mountain hermit had once made his home there and had amused himself by stealthily approaching visitors on the mountains and scaring them out of their wits with his sudden chuckle. Eventually he was found dead in his cave, and the sinister echo of his laughter is reputed to linger on. It's also said that a cold hand touches any interloper's shoulder the moment his light goes out.

The amazing Boomslang Cave, penetrating right through a ridge for 146 m, was discovered in 1911, and it was here that Meyer met a fellow explorer. It was an amusing chance meeting. Meyer started his cave journey from the low northern entrance, wriggling in on his stomach. At the same time, J.C.W. Moore started from the southern side, where the entrance is high and overlooks the Fish Hoek glen. The two men met in one of the chambers in the middle reaches of the cave and, with a candle burning on a ledge of rock, they enjoyed a chat about the mountains and the wonders of the caverns. Moore was a Kalk Bay man who knew the area well, and his knowledge stimulated Meyer to learn more about this fascinating place. As a result of his holiday explorations, Meyer was privileged to discover two new caves which he named Central Grotto and Johles Cave, the latter a combination of his own name and that of a companion, Leslie van Blerk. He never forgot the pleasure of these pioneer explorations. In 1935 he retired, a sick man, but he returned to Kalk Bay and made his home there, determined to devote what time he had left to a study of the mountains and to the discovery of more caverns. During the following

ber of the white-walled homes of the Cape owed their smart appearance to the area's lime. The village had its beginning as a simple outspan along the rough coastal track, but in 1806 Abraham Kloppers, who had started trek fishing in Muizenberg, acquired some ground, built a home and started to catch and dry fish as slave rations. A number of the Filipino sailors also settled at Kalk Bay.

In the days before refrigeration, the making of bokkems (kippers), the drying and salting of snoek and other suitable catches was the only means of preserving fish. The harbour is always a busy place, but around June and July, the peak of the snoek season, it is especially bustling. Catches of 40 000 snoek, landed in a single day in this compact little har-

bour, are not uncommon. Fresh fish is sold in the harbour. There are two small tidal pools.

The mountain massif dominating the Muizenberg to Kalk Bay coastal stretch is a superb recreational area for the energetic walker, cave explorer and nature lover. It is like a gigantic rock garden, ingeniously devised by Nature to shelter a vast variety of flowering plants that display their lovely blooms against a background of splendid views across False Bay. There are paths to most places of interest in these mountains.

Above Kalk Bay, named for former lime ('kalk') kilns, is both a flourishing suburb and working harbour.

Opposite Sturdy line-fishing boats harvest the waters of False Bay, and the catch is sold on the jetty.

months he wandered over the heights and the more he explored, the more he found. The exercise and fresh air gave him a new lease on life.

A small band of friends gathered around Meyer, for he was a most amiable companion on the mountains. Knowledgeable, communicative, humorous, he knew many good yarns and was a fine hand at brewing coffee and grilling a chop. Through their activities, Meyer and his friends became known as the Moles. Meyer was recognised as First Mole. A certificate was awarded to his companions who had explored at least the dozen principal caves of the 95 assorted grottoes, caverns, pits and other exciting places that had been discovered and named, most of them by the energetic Meyer.

The pleasure the Moles had in their various outings is reflected in the names: Rest-a-Bit, Light and Gloom, Six Moles Cave, Moss and Diamonds, Drip-Drop, Sunbeam Cave, Noonday Rest, Mirth Parlour and many more. Some of these have vanished from modern maps but most remain, many painted on the rock walls. Countless later visitors have enjoyed pleasant days of adventurous exercise in rediscovering these interesting places.

The heights of this sandstone mass consists of a number of parallel ridges. The ceaseless dripping and washing of water during the wet months of winter has eroded the rocks into curious shapes (such as the remarkable head overlooking Devil's Pit, which resembles that of a latter-day South African prime minister) and modelled numerous caverns. Of these, the most extensive so far found is Ronan's Well, a cave known before Meyer's time but for many years thought to be only 68 m long. Then a modern cave explorer (or speleologist), Michael McAdam, followed a draught of air coming through a narrow crack and, with some difficult scrambling and a tight 2,5 m long squeeze, opened the way into an involved series of underground chambers, halls and crevices stretching for 365 m into the depth of what is known as Ridge Peak and thence out through two other caves, Aladdin and Robin Hood. Ronan's Well is not a cave for a beginner to explore: even the entrance is tricky – a rather sinister-looking grotto with a dark hole 5,5 m up its inner wall, which takes the explorer into the heart of the mountain.

Boomslang Cave, the second most extensive cave so far found is a safe, exciting 146 m passage through the ridge known as Cave Peak. There are several impressive chambers, a 9 m crawl on the northern end, and an impressive southern exit high over Fish Hoek. It was at the pool on the floor of this exit that the original discoverers disturbed a boomslang ('Tree snake') – hence the name. The third largest cave in these mountains was found by Meyer in 1941, and exploring it must have been thrilling. The first entrance he found was a narrow 9,5 m deep pit, and to descend he needed a rope ladder. At the bottom end of the pit the cave stretches out in a succession of passages and chambers for 132 m. At the southeastern end an easier entrance was later found; a 3,6 m deep chimney connected,

through a low cavern and a narrow passageway, with Annie's Hall, the first of the large caverns. Meyer, who named several of his cave discoveries after figures in classical mythology, called the whole remarkable cave sequence Oread Hall, after the Oreads, the nymphs of caverns and mountains in Greek legend.

Among the numerous parties which Meyer conducted through the caves was one consisting of twenty lady teachers. Getting them through

Above View from Kalk Bay mountainside, which is riddled with caves. Some may yet be undiscovered.

the section of Boomslang Cave, where explorers are forced to crawl, must have taken some coaxing, but generally he seems to have enjoyed having women accompany him on explorations. Several of his discoveries carry names of these friends and acquaintances, such as Pollie's Cave, Beatrice Cave, Nellie's Pool and Dolly's Doorway.

The last cave Meyer and his Moles found was a small cavern rather wistfully named Me Too. After that his health deteriorated and, in 195, broke down completely. He recovered partially, made two more climbs and then died of lung cancer on 9 September 1952. He was 78 years old; the mountains had given him the gift of nineteen healthy years during which his diary records 1 700 climbs into the Kalk Bay mountains. Memories of him will linger over the uplands. In later days Jose Burman and S. MacPherson found a cave on the Red Afrikaner Ridge and fittingly named it Meyer's Memorial.

From Kalk Bay the coastal road continues past the entrance to the harbour and curves around the slopes of the mountains. After 1,5 km a fine view of Fish Hoek and its glen is revealed, with (on the northern side) the residential suburb of Clovelly.

FISH HOEK

Fish Hoek is almost unique in Southern Africa. It's a striking example of non-town-planning, and for nearly two centuries it's been 'dry'! The original grant of the farm Vischhoek ('Fish glen') was made by the Governor, Lord Charles Somerset, to Andries Bruins in 1818. There were conditions to this grant. The farm lay directly on the road to the naval station of Simon's Town and some very thirsty sailors on shore leave. The prudent Somerset therefore stipulated that no public wine house be kept on the farm, a condition perpetuated in the township created in 1919. The municipality grew up as one of the country's few teetotaller centres. You could drink in Fish Hoek from your own supplies but, in the absence of bottle stores and bars, the town boasted a minimal crime rate.

Nowadays there are still no liquor outlets but restaurants and sports clubs are licensed.

The place grew up as a residential area connected by railway to Cape Town. Despite its congested and unbeautiful layout, its dismal absence of trees, and its principal commercial street doubling up as the main coastal road carrying heavy traffic to the southern end of the Cape Peninsula, it is a relaxed, self-contained seaside centre with a safe bathing beach.

The glen in which Fish Hoek lies cuts right across the Cape Peninsula. In comparatively recent geological times (Cretaceous: 65-125 million years ago) the sea washed through, leaving the southern portion of the Peninsula an island. The sandy floor of the glen was once the sea bed. In a great rock shelter overlooking its northern side, prehistoric people once lived and dined on marine molluscs, fish and the tidal life which teemed

in the shallow waters below them. The rock shelter became known as the Schildersgat ('Painter's cave') from the rock art left on its walls by the early inhabitants. It is now more generally known as Peers Cave after Victor Peers and his son Bertram, who in 1926 began a painstaking exploration of the place, which yielded the skull of Fish Hoek Man, a representative of the community which inhabited this part of Southern Africa 15 000 years ago, or perhaps even earlier.

Peers Cave may be reached by following the road from Fish Hoek through the glen to the western side of the Peninsula. At 3,5 km from the centre of Fish Hoek, there is a sign indicating the turn-off to the sports ground and to the cave. From the end of this road there is a path through a forest of Port Jackson trees, then over glistening white sand dunes and up the slopes of the ridge to Peers and to the remarkable Tunnel Cave, in which interesting artefacts have also been found.

The beach at Fish Hoek slopes gently and provides safe swimming. The pleasant Jager Walk winds its way through the rocks at the water's edge. In the beach restaurant there is an interesting memento of the trek fishermen of yesteryear: the 19th century Filipino fishermen who started the industry. The first boat they used, the *Bonita*, was overturned in a False Bay

Above left Trek fishermen and passersby discuss prospects on the wide expanse of Fish Hoek beach.

storm and the crew were drowned. The prow of the boat now stands as the centrepiece of the restaurant, a mute memorial to a sad tragedy, kept in a place that specialises in seafood.

SIMON'S TOWN

From Fish Hoek, the main road passes the small residential area of Glencairn, a kilometre beyond which is the Dido Valley Road turn-off. A short way along this road is Topstones, more familiar to Capetonians and visitors as The Scratch Patch, the world's largest gemstone-tumbling factory. It has interesting origins: in 1967 Bruce Baines finished his training as a lawyer in Cape Town, but decided not to enter practice. His interest lay in gemstones and in the creation of beautiful things. He went to London and established a gemstone manufacturing and distributing business.

Then fate took a hand in the game. Bruce secured a contract to provide Mobil Europe with 40 million gemstones for use in a free-gift promotional scheme in garages. To produce these Bruce, his brother and two other partners had to set up a factory. The contract called for the gemstones known as tiger's eye to be a substantial part of the 40 million stones. Tiger's eye is of South African origin, and a law forbade its export in unfinished form. There had to be a tumbling plant in South Africa, and Simon's Town was the choice.

Such was the beginning of Topstones. Since its creation countless thousands of beautiful gemstones have been tumbled, polished and mounted in the factory. Outside there is a treasure-hunter's delight, a patch where fossickers have a real chance of finding all manners of lovely things amongst thousands of fragments of gemstones. The Scratch Patch also has a branch at the Waterfront.

The main coastal road, after another kilometre, reaches Simon's Town, spectacularly situated beneath a 678 m high ridge of mountains. Governor

Simon van der Stel recommended its development, in 1687, as an alternative winter sanctuary to Table Bay, which was exposed to northwesterly storms, and it was named Simon's Bay in his honour. A wooden pier, barracks and two small forts were built in 1743, and in 1814 it became a naval base for the British South Atlantic Squadron. Substantial workshops and a dry dock were constructed , and it is from this time that Simon's Town, with its narrow, twisting streets, acquired something of the special naval atmosphere of a small English seafaring centre. The handsome Admiralty House, which had initially done duty as lodgings, was taken over by the British as the residence of the Commander-in-Chief. The South African Navy assumed control of the naval base in 1957.

Simon's Town is the home port for over 200 private ocean-going yachts and power boats, many used by their owners to pursue big game-fish (tunny and marlin) during the summer season off the Cape of Good Hope. The False Bay Yacht Club, which incorporates the South African Marlin and Tuna Club, has its quarters close to the harbour. The South African record bluefin tunny stands at 361 kg, and was caught by Brian Cohen in December 1968.

Simon's Town is the terminus of the suburban railway from Cape Town, and a stroll down the main street is a rewarding experience: like Muizenberg, it has its Historic Mile of period buildings and heritage sites. The Simon's Town Museum, in the original Residency used by the Governor on his periodic visits, contains a varied collection of intrguing relics from Simon's Town's past. One section is devoted to the celebrated dog 'Just Nuisance', who was a great friend of the British sailors during the Second World War. He died in Simon's Town in April 1944 at the age of just seven and is buried above the town. A bronze memorial to him stands in Jubilee Square in the centre of the town, where he often helped collect money for charity. The original police cells, including a 'black hole' (punishment cell), are in the museum's basement. Next door is the South African Naval Museum, where you can see ship models, a hands-on operations room, the bridge of a submarine and of a minesweeper.

Another interesting building is the Martello Tower, built in 1796 by the British who, after seizing the Cape, needed to guard it against possible invasion by Napoleon's forces. The tower was a copy of a French fortification which had caused the British no little grief when, in 1794, they set out to capture the bay of Florenzo in Corsica as a base for their blockade of port of Toulon. The British had never encountered such a fortification. It was deceptively simple, just a circular tower of stone garrisoned by two grenadiers, twenty seamen and armed with two cannon. Two British warships were soundly repelled by the fortification, which stood on Cape Mortella. The two ships were severely damaged before the disgruntled British withdrew from the resolute little fort. It took a land attack, launched the next morning, to subdue the tower, and then only by smoking the defenders out by setting fire to damp wood piled around the sides.

The Martello Tower stands on naval property but may be visited by arrangement. A stone wall with a gate surrounds the tower. On the slopes overlooking Simon's Town stand several historic old gun batteries, including the Scala Battery of three 9,2 inch (23,2 cm) calibre guns, capable of firing a projectile for nearly 40 km. Even older is the Zoutman Battery with a 9 inch (22,8 cm) muzzle-loading gun built in 1890. Numerous ruins of old fortifications can be seen.

THE ROAD SOUTH

The main coastal road leaves Simon's Town (and the last petrol point for 55 km) and continues to the end of the Peninsula along a stretch of coast that is best described as one long ocean playground. Here are delectable

Left A colony of endemic African (previously Jackass) penguins at home on the beach at Boulders.
Opposite Simon's Town was fondly known as 'Snoekie' by the Royal Navy, which occupied it from 1814 until 1957.

little bathing places such as Seaforth and Boulders, which are sheltered from the winds of summer. Seaforth was named by an early settler, Captain Harington, whose wife was a niece of the Earl of Seaforth.

A pathway links Seaforth to Boulders, where a protected colony of penguins lives among the gigantic granite boulders and mixes on sociable terms with human beings. Other delightful bathing places in this area include Windmill Beach, Water's Edge Beach, Fisherman's Beach, Foxy Beach and Froggy Pond.

Above A profusion of flowering fynbos covers the windswept flats near Cape Point.

The highlight of this stretch of coast comes 8 km from Simon's Town, at Miller's Point. In 1828 this beautiful locality was acquired by Edmund Miller, who built a seaside cottage there called Elsemere. Until 1850 his family had the whole place to themselves and he conducted whaling operations in False Bay, mainly during the winter months when female southern rights and humpback or fin whales habitually come into False Bay to calve. Then the estate passed into other hands. Today Miller's Point is a fine public coastal resort. In this superb setting, the then Cape Divisional Council imaginatively created a caravan park, with vehicles deployed on terraces that enjoy a view of sea and distant mountains which no luxury hotel could surpass. Playgrounds, boat-launching facilities, a restaurant, a large tidal swimming-pool, green lawns, innumerable picnic spots and a profusion of wild flowers are among the attractions of this recreational area. For the canoeist and underwater swimmer there is a glorious garden beneath the ocean, with anemones and sea urchins of brilliant hues set in waving forests of seaweed, among which shoals of lively fish wander like butterflies in a magical world.

From Miller's Point the road continues south along the coast for a further 5 km, passing many picnic spots and viewsites until, gaining steadily in height, it climbs diagonally along the cliffs 91 m above the bay known as Smitswinkel ('The blacksmith's shop'), a name suggested by a pair of rocks in the sea, one shaped like an anvil, the other like a bellows. Smitswinkel Bay is a favourite fishing spot, with a cluster of informal shacks built on the water's edge, where their owners enjoy a happy privacy. Troops of baboons frequent this portion of the road. Human visitors are warned that it is an offence to feed wild animals. Baboons are amusing to watch but they can become nasty if they are tempted to climb onto cars by handouts of food.

The road now swings away from the coast, and after 8 km reaches a junction with a turn-off to the left, taking the traveller for the final 13 km southwards to Cape Point. This final stretch leads through the Cape of Good Hope Nature Reserve.

THE CAPE OF GOOD HOPE

A visit to the Cape of Good Hope Nature Reserve at the tip of the Peninsula makes a most fascinating outing. The area has excellent roads and is easily accessible at all seasons of the year. The summer months (November to March) are inclined to be windy. The winter months (May to August) are pleasant, as the rainfall is hardly sufficient to disturb visitors for more than a few days each year. Spring (September and October), when the countryside is strewn with wild flowers, is particularly lovely.

Top Engagingly human-like baboons may also be vicious and resentful. Do not feed!

Walking trails lead to many pleasant and secluded places. At Buffel's Bay and Bordjiesrif there are enclosed tidal swimming-pools and at Buffel's Bay a launching ramp for boats. Other amenities include picnic spots and a field museum. Most tourists to the region visit the reserve. The end of the road at Cape Point, in fact, is one of the most famous coach terminuses in the world.

At this stage it is perhaps appropriate to clarify a persistent controversy about the waters washing the two sides of the Peninsula. Are they those of the Indian Ocean or those of the Atlantic Ocean? In actual fact the sea knows no oceans. Man, for the sake of geographical convenience, has applied a variety of names to portions of the sea, but the straight lines he draws between them are just as imaginary as the thread stretched across the lens of a telescope by sailors and shown as the equator to gullible passengers when they first cross the famous 'line'.

The sea knows only the differences of temperature and currents in its various parts, and these are the decisive influences affecting all forms of marine life. When the first sailors came down the west coast searching for an end to Africa and a sea route to the east, they discovered that the peninsula of the Cape of Good Hope was the most southwesterly point. It was not the most southerly point – that is Cape Agulhas, 170 km eastwards – but it was to them the most important, for on doubling it, they not only began the great swing eastwards, but changes in water temperature and marine life confirmed that they were entering a new world. No such significant changes were discernible on either side of Cape Agulhas at any season of the year. It was the Cape of Good Hope, which marked the blending of the cultures and life forms of East and West. It is here that two powerful currents of this part of the sea – the warm Mozambique-Agulhas coming down the east coast and the cold Antarctic Drift which forms the Benguela Current running up the west coast of Africa – have their collision course. The warm waters of the east finally lose themselves, but by their pressure ensure that the cold waters sweep on up the west coast and do not penetrate eastwards.

Few fish or other forms of marine life can tolerate a temperature change of 5°C or more in water. To the warm-water Indo-Pacific species living on the east side of Africa, and the cold-water species living on the southwest side, the difference between the two currents provides a barrier as impenetrable as a garden wall.

The Cape of Good Hope is always the beacon. It is one of the great landmarks of the world, proclaiming that this is where the two halves of the globe, East and West, merge; where two ways of life have their frontiers and blend with the culture of the great dividing continent of Africa. It

Opposite The old Cape Point lighthouse was replaced by another, closer to sea level.

is here that two major ocean currents, each with an enormous influence on all forms of life, climate and scenery in their proximity, have a rendezvous and, simultaneously, a parting of the ways.

Luis de Camões, the poet genius of Portugal, tells of the legendary origin of the Cape Peninsula in the majestic verse of his *Lusiads*. The monstrous Adamastor ('The untamed') was one of the 100 giants who rebelled against the gods of ancient Greece and attempted to take Mount Olympus by storm. Defeated by Hercules and Vulcan at the head of all the gods, the giants were condemned to eternal punishment. They were banished to the far places of Earth and buried under volcanoes and mountains.

Adamastor, the personification of the perceived barbarism of ancient Africa, was consigned to a special transmutation. It is his body 'turned to rocks all rough and strange' which forms the peninsula of the Cape of Good Hope. His spirit forever haunts this tomb. With Table Mountain as his workshop for storms and thunderbolts, he roams the surrounding seas in the form of howling gales and dark storm-clouds, roaring dire vengeance on the sailors who disturb his seclusion. The pioneer Portuguese explorers were the sailors who first dared Adamastor's rage. The vengeance which he cursed upon them persists, as may be seen in the strange tale of the *Flying Dutchman*.

THE STORY OF THE CAPE

Apart from leaving a few middens, prehistoric human beings played no significant part in the story of the Cape Peninsula. Their ancient garbage dumps may still be seen at places such as Batsata Cove, Cape Maclear, Bonteberg and Rooikrans, where there was some natural shelter from the winds and where drinking-water was available from springs.

Early human beings in these areas collected shellfish and lobsters, caught various fish species, foraged for bulbs, roots and edible vegetation, and hunted and trapped game in close competition with other resident predators, such as the now-extinct Cape lion and the lynx. There were probably not many game animals.

The winds of the Cape Peninsula made life unpleasant for the larger mammals and the absence in the soil of such essentials to their welfare as copper traces made the grazing unpalatable. Migrating animals which wandered about at will could visit the area seasonally but leave when they tired of the winds and poor grazing. Such migrants could have included Cape buffalo, elephant, black rhino and various antelope. Baboons were always present. They are today a source of amusement to all visitors and of interest to scientists in that they scavenge the beaches in search of sea foods in similar manner to prehistoric humans.

Opposite 'The Fairest Cape' with the cold Atlantic Ocean in the foreground, and False Bay in the distance.

Bird life was varied, with about 150 species resident at different seasons of the year. A variety of sea-birds was always the principal feature. Jackass penguins (now renamed African penguins) landed on the beaches, while albatrosses, giant petrels, gannets, black-backed gulls, Hartlaub's gulls and cormorants were all common around the coast. Of the land birds, the malachite and orange-breasted sunbirds were the most striking.

In the surrounding sea, Cape sea-lions, whales, porpoises, sharks, tunny, yellowtail and snoek were in abundance. On land, tortoises have always been common. The Cape of Good Hope Nature Reserve is, in fact, one of their great breeding grounds. A few Cape cobras, boomslangs, puffadders and other snakes also made their homes in the southern Peninsula.

The modern history of the Cape of Good Hope began in a howling gale, which blew in the last three weeks of January 1488 and which concealed, according to Luis de Camões, the sullen fury of the giant Adamastor. Down the west coast, probing, searching for the end of Africa, came the Portuguese explorer Bartholomeu Dias in a cramped cockleshell of a ship with a sick and frightened crew.

On 6 January 1488, off the southwest coast, they saw the lovely Cederberg range and named it 'Mountains of the Three Magi Kings'. Then another storm enveloped them. The tiny ship was blown far from land, with Dias pitting his own resolution against the full force of Nature. At last, as the storm abated, the sailors looked for land to the east, but found nothing save the swirling sea. The ship swung northwards. In the storm they had unknowingly rounded the tip of Africa. Only on 3 February 1488 did they reach land at what is now known as Mossel Bay. The unseen cape around which they had found their way they named the Cabo Tormentoso (Cape of Storms).

Dias sailed on, with his crew in a mutinous and sulky mood but beyond Algoa Bay, off the mouth of the Chalumna River, they were forced to turn back, leaving a stone pillar erected on a lonely headland known as the 'Rock of the Fountains'. At least the weather was fine, however. Keeping close to the coast, they discovered Cape Agulhas, naming it 'Cape St Brendan', as it was on the feast day of St Brendan (16 May), that they passed it.

A few days later they passed Cape Hangklip, looked into the spacious and lovely 'Gulf Within the Mountains' (False Bay); and then, in fair and gentle weather at last, the Portuguese historian Barros wrote, 'they beheld that great and remarkable Cape hidden for so many centuries, which when discovered revealed not itself alone, but another world of lands'. To this the Portuguese king eventually gave the new name Cape of Good Hope (applied to the whole cape, not simply to one point upon it). Dias spent a month anchored somewhere off its shores, resting his crew, writing his reports and perfecting a map of his voyage. Then, leaving

another stone cross (no trace of which has ever been found despite dedicated searching), he sailed for home.

In the renaming of the Cape of Good Hope, Dias conveniently forgot his earlier 'Cape of Storms', but it – and the vengeance of Adamastor – did not forget him. In 1500 he once again set out to double the Cape of Good Hope. Again he encountered a terrible storm and this time his ship and a companion vessel were overwhelmed. They both lie somewhere in the deep waters of the southern sea. Legend has it that in this disaster Adamastor had his revenge; and so the tale arose of a phantom sea captain and his ship, condemned forever in his attempt to round the Cape of Good Hope, but always frustrated by violent storms. The nationality of the unfortunate individual has varied with the telling through the years. Wagner, in his opera The Flying Dutchman, favoured the Dutch version, with Captain Van der Decken as the central character whose fate was redeemed by the constancy of a woman. But fundamentally the tale is rooted in the curse of Adamastor's fury and his vengeance on Bartholomeu Dias. This feud continues forever. It is in fact astonishing how many sailors navigating these waters have made serious reports about a sighting of the phantom ship. It is the world's most famous ghost story.

Since the time of its discovery, the Cape of Good Hope has remained a point of great interest to all voyagers. East- and west-bound travellers alike regard it as the half-way mark on their journreys. To double it in a storm is an achievement comparable to doubling Cape Horn. To sail around it in fair weather is a delightful experience. From the tiny 100 ton Golden Hind, Sir Francis Drake in the course of his round-the-world odyssey (1577 to 1580) saw it. In his log it is described as 'the fairest cape and the most stately thing we saw in the whole circumference of the globe'. Few disagree with this description.

A LIGHT IN THE DARKNESS
In the early years the southern part of the Peninsula was a windswept wilderness of wild flowers. A few fishermen and runaways from justice occasionally made their way down to the tip of the Cape, but there were no roads and no settlement in the area until the first quarter of the 19th century, when the British took control of the Cape and Simon's Town was developed as a naval base.

Farms were then allocated in the area. But nothing was done about a lighthouse for some years, although the need for a beacon became increasingly urgent as the volume of shipping around the Cape increased. In 1823 the coastline was properly surveyed by Royal Navy chartists, among them a Captain Owen, and names were given to the various rocks,

Opposite Dias Beach is named for an early explorer who sailed around the Cape.

including Bellows (the dangerous outlying rock, always covered in foam), Anvil, Whittle (in False Bay) and Dias Reef. Captain Owen, incidentally, also reported sighting the Flying Dutchman.

The first lighthouse, a prefabricated iron tower painted white with a red top, was erected in 1859 on Da Gama peak, the summit of Cape Point, 249 m above sea-level. Made by the Victoria Foundry Company in England, this was 9 m high with a 2 000 candlepower flashing light. The first lighthouse keepers soon found that their lamp was too high. When the mists swept in, the light was often well above the clouds and quite invisible to any shipping. This created a dangerous situation, but for some time nothing was done to rectify matters.

A few farmers had established themselves on land in the southern Peninsula, but little is remembered of them. With bad roads, thin soil and incessant wind, they were forced to live on a subsistence economy. Horses, however, flourished in the area. The farmers managed to grow some barley and wheat. Milk and vegetables were produced for the shipping at Simon's Town. A few homesteads were built of local sandstone cemented with lime made from shells in the kilns at Buffel's Bay and Bordjiesrif. Remnants of the homesteads may still be seen, but memories of the personalities who lived in them and the events which took place have long since been blown away with the winds.

Occasionally a shipwreck occurred somewhere around the coast, and there were sightings of the Flying Dutchman. One of the most famous of these was logged in 1881 by the future King George V when he was a midshipman on HMS Bacchante. The lighthouse keepers also reported sightings of odd vessels, with all sails set even in the worst weather, persistently trying to double the Cape. Even the coming of steamships did not end these tales of sea ghosts.

On the night of 18 April 1911 a major disaster occurred when the 5 557 ton Portuguese liner Lusitania struck Bellows Rock. The lighthouse of Cape Point was completely obscured by the mist. The ship was a total loss, although fortunately only four out of the 774 people aboard were drowned. This disaster tragically emphasised the urgency of a change to the lighthouse. It was recorded that in some years the light was obscured by mist for as much as 900 hours. This was an intolerable situation.

A new site was selected lower down on the tip of Cape Point, only 87 m above the sea and overlooking the strange column known as Dias Rock, which stands guard there as though watching eternally for a return of Dias's vanished ship. On 25 April 1914 the foundation was laid for the new lighthouse and in due course a 500 000 candlepower paraffin lamp installed. In 1936 this lamp was converted to electricity, with a giant reflector and lens providing 19 000 000 candlepower, making the lighthouse the most powerful in the world. This light was later reduced to 10 000 000 candlepower provided by a 1,5 kw lamp.

The light at Cape Point can justly be described as one of the greatest shipping beacons in the world. Countless sailors have been guided by its tremendous beam. The giant tankers which make their way around the Cape, rusty freighters, trim ocean liners, pugnacious warships, sneaky submarines on the prowl – all regard it as a massive landmark. During the Second World War German U-Boats lurked by day beneath the waters and by night lay on the restless surface just beyond the beam of light, waiting patiently for prey.

Several of these nocturnal prowlers reported sightings of the Flying Dutchman. Just before the war, in early 1939, crowds of holiday makers on False Bay beaches reported a weird-looking battered old sailing-ship making its way towards Muizenberg and then vanishing in a cloud of mist. This intriguing legend persists into modern times. It is a colourful part of the character and romantic atmosphere of the Cape of Good Hope, the commanding presence of which dominates one of the great strategic trade routes of the world.

THE MAKING OF A SANCTUARY
The idea of preserving the southern portion of the Cape Peninsula as a nature reserve originated in 1928, when the whole area was threatened with development – with seaside resorts complete with 'Trespassers will be Prosecuted' signs and forlorn, dilapidated holiday shacks deserted for months at a time.

Fortunately several public-spirited and influential Capetonians became interested in the area. Brian Mansergh, a Cape Town architect, had known it since his youth and had often discussed its conservation with local farmers. In November 1928 he wrote to the Minister of Lands, pleading for the establishment of a nature reserve. His plea was rejected on the grounds of cost. Mansergh continued to promote the idea of a reserve, supported by a number of friends, who gathered for a weekly informal lunch during which they discussed affairs in general and the southern tip of the Peninsula in particular. News of the formation of a syndicate to develop townships in the area particularly disturbed them. A patient spell of propaganda and some systematic agitation followed. Dr Stacy Skaife, Dr Leonard Gill, Anthony Leyds and Henry Hope concentrated on arousing public interest. The key property in the area was Smith's Farm, owned by Norman Smith and his family. This was actually the farm Buffelsfontein or Uiterstehoek, originally granted to John Osmond, extending across the end of the Peninsula. The Smith family was approached. They approved the idea of conservation and agreed to sell to the conservationists rather than to the land speculators.

The City Council was then approached, but the area was well outside their boundaries and individual councillors were not enthusiastic. One of them, A.Z. Berman, summed up resistance to the idea by stating flatly that

he would be against spending council money on an area where 'there was not enough vegetation to keep a scorpion alive'. Another councillor described it as 'wasteland, waterless and treeless'.

The enthusiasts were not dismayed. They started to make plans for raising the money to buy Smith's Farm, fence it in, and make it pay for its maintenance as a nature reserve by erecting a toll-gate on the road leading across it to the lighthouse and to resorts such as Buffel's Bay and the famous fishing ledges at Rooikrans, places much frequented by visitors.

At this stage Will and Percy Hare, owners of the farm Bloubergvlei, which was also in the area, offered their property to the projected nature reserve – provided that it would be maintained as a wilderness and that they would be allowed to live undisturbed in their seaside cottage at Brightwater, and that no road would ever be built across what had been their land. The whole concept of a nature reserve gained in stature. The Simon's Town municipality supported the idea. Its mayor, L.C. Gay, was particularly enthusiastic. The local morning newspaper, the *Cape Times*, gave it considerable editorial support. One memorable leader (23 November 1938) was amusingly specific: 'It seems almost treasonable to this stately peninsula of ours to think that its extreme end, now the only unspoilt part of our heritage, should fall into the hands of men who will cause it to pimple into a bungaloid acne'.

The City Council, however, remained hostile, although a poll of the people of Cape Town revealed overwhelming support. Charles Duminy, chairman of the Divisional Council of the Cape, and Jerwyn Owen, its secretary, had fortunately also been interested in the project for some time. They put it to their council and the idea was at last officially accepted. On 11 April 1939, a special meeting approved the purchase of Smith's Farm. The Cape of Good Hope Nature Reserve came into being, with the specific object of preserving for all time the 'fairest Cape' in the state in which it must have been seen by Bartholomeu Dias and Sir Francis Drake. Norman Smith was appointed first warden with £250 a year as salary and free occupation of his farmhouse.

The Divisional Council spent £16 000 in purchasing Smith's Farm with its homestead and three privately owned bungalows. Crown land was added by the State. In 1941 the farms Olifantsbos, Theefontein and Krommerivier were bought from the estate of D.C. de Villiers, as well as the Minicki family farm, Klaasjagers. Other land was acquired to consolidate the area. The last property to be purchased (in 1965) was a portion of Wildschutsbrand, owned by Mrs Jacoba Malherbe. This farm had been the first to be granted in the southern Peninsula – originally (in the 1660s) it had been the home of the first field-cornet, or district officer, appointed over the area. The homesteads of all these farms have vanished, including, unfortunately, the one known locally as Die Spookhuis ('The haunted house'), a building with quite a number of tales about its unorthodox residents.

With this acquisition, the Cape of Good Hope Nature Reserve attained its present dimension of 7 750 ha, obtained by the Divisional Council of the Cape at a total cost of £63 500. Completely protected and carefully maintained, it is a scenic and botanical delight. Game animals of the type which once roamed freely over the Southern Cape (eland, bontebok, hartebeest and mountain zebra) have been re-introduced. These, together with descendants of the indigenous population of grey rhebok, grysbok, steenbok, baboons, marine life, over 1 200 species of birds, dassies, tortoises (especially the Cape angulated tortoise) and other small wild creatures, live their natural lives in a setting which is peaceful, beautiful, and quite unique.

The original homestead of Smith's Farm was converted into a restaurant and gift shop to cater for an increasing stream of visitors. In 1994 the number of annual visitors reached 443 500. To cope with such numbers, a lease agreement was negotiated in 1995 with Concor Holdings (Pty) Limited for the self-financed construction and management of a modern complex of buildings and also the construction of a funicular railway to convey visitors from the road terminus to the viewsite on the summit of Cape Point. At the end of this lease, the ownership of this complex, including a restaurant, gift shop, information centre and funicular railway, reverts back to the Cape Metropolitan Council. The funicular track is 585 metres long and ascends 230 metres. The two coaches each have a capacity of 40 passengers and take three minutes to complete the journey. They replace a bus known as the *Flying Dutchman* which originally provided a service for those disinclined to do the walk. Utmost care was

Above The steel tower of Slangkop lighthouse has guided ocean traffic since 1914.

taken to preserve the environment during construction and many restrictions were placed on the developer with regards to the positioning of the funicular track, thus resulting in one of the most unique layouts accommodating varying gradients and curves.

In 1998 the number of visitors exceeded 750 000. It was apparent that a trip to the Cape of Good Hope was becoming an essential part of any tour of South Africa by international visitors.

There is also a good walkway to the summit, with viewsites and resting places en route. The original buildings, including the first lighthouse, have been restored. Since 1978 the South African Council for Scientific and Industrial Research (CSIR) have maintained on the summit an atmospheric trace gas research station with a laboratory, facilities and a 30 m high aluminium mask to provide experimental platforms and stratified air intakes. This facility is managed jointly by the CSIR and the IFU (Frauhofer Institute for Atmospheric Environmental Research) in Germany. It is part of the World Meteorological Organisation Global Atmosphere Watch Network. There are nineteen similar facilities maintained at strategic situations around the world. They keep a close, continuous watch on trace gases in the atmosphere, meteorological conditions and solar radiation.

Altogether the Cape of Good Hope Nature Reserve, with its fauna, flora, spectacular scenery, atmosphere and ongoing activity, is a very worthwhile place to visit and a credit to the staff who maintain it. The reserve forms part of the Cape Peninsula National park.

SCARBOROUGH AND KOMMETJIE

From the turn-off leading into the reserve, the main road commences its journey back to Cape Town up the west coast of the Peninsula. Carvings, crafts and curios are sold by wayside vendors. There are pleasant picnic sites beneath the trees on either side of the road and an ostrich show farm. At 8,5 km towards Cape Town, close to the junction with the road coming from Simon's Town over Red Hill, the farm Perdekloof ('Horse ravine') has been converted into a recreational area with shady trees and green grass, ideal for a picnic.

A further 3 km takes the road past Scarborough, which consists of a cluster of cottages close to the oddly shaped roadside landmark known as Camel Rock. There is a pretty beach. When the wind is not blowing, the picnic and camping sites are pleasant.

For 7,5 km beyond Scarborough the country is wild and bush-covered, with sandy bays such as Witsand ('White sands') and many picnic sites and camping grounds in sheltered places along the way. After 5 km there is a crossroads with a turn-off left which leads to the recreational area of Soetwater ('Sweet water'). A right turn provides a short cut through the housing estate of Ocean View to Fish Hoek. The main road now climbs to reveal a large stretch of coast with tidal pools, the Soetwater park and a

recreational area dominated by the graceful steel tower of Slangkop ('Snake peak') lighthouse.

The road now descends into the pleasant little resort known as Kommetjie ('Little basin'), which takes its name from a natural inlet in the rocks that has been developed into a large tidal pool. This area is a favourite place for surf riders, as is Long Beach, especially in the summer months when the southeaster is blowing. The view north towards Chapman's Peak and Hout Bay is particularly impressive from here. Swimming in the tidal pool is safe and the water is relatively warm.

Holidaymakers discovered the charms of the area, especially fishing and swimming, in the late 1800s. A few shacks were put up to provide more

Above Noordhoek's Long Beach is a great surfing beach when the south-easter blows.

substantial shelter than the milkwood trees, and then the inevitable developer arrived, determined that if the public showed signs of liking the area, they could be induced to buy plots. A company, Kommetjie Estate Ltd, was formed in 1902 by a Cape Town builder and contractor, who had the resort named Kommetjie laid out. A gravel road was built to Fish Hoek, its verges planted with the diverse-coloured flowering gums which make the route so beautiful in spring.

the high waves today. The ship was cut down and stripped of its valuables and plates. The ribs, keel and boiler remain to form a picturesque scene, used in modern times as a set in several motion picture films, including *Ryan's Daughter*.

A wreck that attracted very large crowds to the salvage auctions held on the beach was the *Clan Monroe*, which struck the rocks just south of the basin on 2 July 1905. Fortunately the crew were all saved except for one man, a Lascar named Ormel Corsette, who was drowned while being taken ashore in a breeches buoy. He is buried on a sand dune near the Slangkop lighthouse. The ship carried a lethal amount of dynamite and cyanide destined for the mines, but there were other valuables aboard and these were auctioned on the beach.

The Slangkop lighthouse was built in 1914, a twin of the lighthouse on Dassen Island – a graceful steel tower in the classic lighthouse shape. The two towers were made in Britain and shipped out to South Africa in pieces. The Slangkop lighthouse was originally fitted with a lamp of 16 750 000 candlepower, making it the second most powerful on the coast of Africa after Cape Point.

During the Second World War a radar station was built on top of the Slangkop ridge, with a tracking leading to the concrete 'pillbox' buildings. The track can still be followed. As with the walk along the beach to the wreck of the *Kakapo*, the walk up to Slangkop ridge provides a pleasant outing. The wild flowers on the ridge are varied and very beautiful, especially in spring.

The route from the village up the ridge leads past St Joseph's Church in Rubbi Road. This charming little church was erected in 1948 as a memorial to Joseph Rubbi, an Italian builder who lived, worked and died in Kommetjie. The church is notable for its marble and mosaics. Behind it stands a building used as a retreat by Catholic nuns and priests.

North of Kommetjie the road leads, as noted, through an avenue of flowering gums. After 1 km it turns off to the left to the Imhoff Park caravan park and to the beach at Klein Slangkoppunt ('Little snake peak point'), from where there is a good walk up the beach of Chapman's Bay to the wreck of the *Kakapo*, now more than half buried in the sand.

NOORDHOEK AND CHAPMAN'S PEAK

After 7 km the road north reaches the suburb of Sun Valley and a junction with the Ou Kaapse Weg (see page 76). Bear left and you will get to Noordhoek ('North glen'), a rural settlement with two attractive little shopping centres – the Kakapo and Noordhoek Village – shaded by oak trees, and situated just below Chapman's Peak. From the main road a side road turns off through the trees, passes the tea-room and leads down to the beach. When the southeaster blows, there are superb surfing waves at De Hoek ('The corner'), where the beach ends on the steep slopes of

A few of the cottages built in those days still survive. Even a railway was planned, but after 85 years the first train has still to arrive. Visitors come by car through the avenue of flowering gums, with the modern tarmac road following substantially the same route as the original track from Fish Hoek. It is a pleasant and pretty drive.

Apart from fishing, surfing and swimming, attractions in the early days included shipwrecks. Back in May 1900 the *Kakapo* was steered directly on to Long Beach. The ship was brand-new and on its maiden delivery from British builders to New Zealand owners. It was named after the rare species of flightless owl parrot of New Zealand. The reason why the wreck occurred is a little obscure. The weather was fine. The navigator said that a sad error had been made: the Sentinel peak at Hout Bay had been mis-taken for the Cape of Good Hope. But even if there had been no confusion, a similar sharp turn around the Cape of Good Hope would hardly have taken the ship to New Zealand. Knowing what goes on when crews of ships stop for refreshment in Table Bay, it is a wonder more of them don't end up on Long Beach!

The crew of the *Kakapo* experienced little hardship as a result of the wreck. The ship went straight onto thick sand; the crew jumped over the side and walked away. The vessel couldn't do the same, however, and was left to settle high and dry on that magnificent beach where surfers ride

Above Chapman's Peak Drive – an outstanding scenic coastal drive – will be reopened as a toll road.

Chapman's Peak. There is some fine walking along the great beach which skirts the bay all the way up to Kommetjie. The name 'Chapman', applied both to the bay and to the dominant peak on the north side, originated on 29 July 1607 when the *Consort*, under Captain David Middleton, anchored off this coast. The master's mate, John Chapman, was sent in a boat to see if there was any anchorage.

In a lovely grove of milkwood and other shady trees there is a secluded cluster of mountainside cottages constructed in what is known as Monkey Valley. Each cottage is different, each has its own character. Each has a superb view of Chapman's Bay with its 8 km long beach. It is a private nature reserve with one of the finest of all forests of the protected milkwood tree permanently defended from the woodcutter's axe. A multitude of birds and a variety of small mammals find sanctuary in it.

The original owner of this 4-ha paradise was an immigrant from the Netherlands named Jan Hesterman. Tradition has it that one day he saw a troop of baboons gambolling up the ravine. Unaware of the difference between baboon and monkey, he called his farm Monkey Valley. In 1988 Monkey Valley was sold by his two sons to Jude Sole, who was enthralled with the beauty of it all, the murmur of the surf and the song of the birds, and determined that this beautiful place should not be defaced by any injudicious property development.

In this way was born the concept of an exclusive resort for a limited number of people sharing the pleasure of living in so sylvan a setting, each having the power to veto further development. Delightfully romantic log tree-houses and thatched brick cottages, all with spectacular views, were built in the forest overlooking the sea. Two private paths lead down to the unspoilt beach. Monkey Valley borders the world-famous Chapman's Peak scenic drive.

For the next 11 km the main road follows one of the world's most spectacular marine drives, cut into the cliffs around the 650 m high Chapman's Peak. This famous scenic road was the brainchild of Sir Frederic de Waal, the same energetic first Administrator of the Cape Province after whom De Waal Drive was named. Stimulated by his enthusiasm, the road was built between 1915 and 1922 and still remains an engineering feat of the first magnitude. It has been a toll road since 2004.

From this road, with its numerous look-out points and picnic places, there are incomparable views back over the great beach of Chapman's Bay and north across the handsome sweep of Hout Bay to the 330 m high Sentinel which looms over the busy fishing harbour. The road itself, for most of its journey around Chapman's Peak, has been cut into the junction line of the Cape granite and the sedimentary Table Mountain sandstone laid down on top of the granite and brilliantly coloured in layers of red, orange and yellow silt, with some dark lines of manganese ore appearing in between the layers.

HOUT BAY

At the end of this great drive the road descends with a grand sweep into the residential and fishing village of Hout Bay. 'Village', however, may be a misnomer: the place has grown enormously in recent years.

Soon after his arrival in the Cape in 1652, Jan van Riebeeck sent a party to explore the bay behind Table Mountain. The explorers found it to be a scenically beautiful, but dangerously exposed for shipping. In the valley there were mountain cypress trees (*Widdringtonia noeliflora*), and from their presence the bay was named Houtbaai ('Wood bay'). Over the years

Above Hout Bay village and harbour are tucked into the Peninsula's mountain chain.

the trees were cut down to supply timber for ships. In 1681 a lease was given over the area, a sawmill built and a wagon track made to the bay over Constantia Nek. A community of woodcutters settled in the area but for some years it remained remote and wild. The last two elephants there were shot in 1689. A few fishermen started to work from the bay, however, and it became regarded as an interesting possible expansion of the settlement at Cape Town.

During the American War of Independence, the French troops who garrisoned the Cape built a battery on the western end of the harbour to defend the place from any possible British invasion. A second battery was built on the eastern side in 1793. Two years later British troops occupied the Cape and built a blockhouse above the eastern battery. In 1804 the

The bronze leopard mounted on the rocks overlooking the bay is the work of the late sculptor, Ivan Mitford-Barberton, who lived in Hout Bay. There are daily launch trips around the bay and to the seals living on Duiker Island, together with sunset cruises to Cape Town and other sea trips on the pleasure launches and sailing craft. There are also some fine walks around Hout Bay, especially that from the harbour over the saddle of land connecting the Sentinel to the mainland. Duiker Island, with its resident population of seals, may be viewed from this walk. From the harbour, too, a disused road climbs steeply to the old radar station built during the Second World War on top of the 653 m high Karbonkelberg. The views are stunning. For the really hardy there is a rough and surprisingly long walk along the coast to Llandudno. With its crevices and hard going, this is a day-long outing, even though it looks short on the map. It is dangerous and should not be undertaken without a guide.

Hout Bay is renowned as the rock lobster capital of the world. During the oppressive apartheid years of sanctions, the place was jocularly proclaimed a 'republic', independent of the rest of South Africa, with its own benign president, an authentic-looking passport, border posts, and a viable economy based on seafoods and the tourists attracted by the excellent eating and the scenic beauty of the area.

Harbours, whatever their size, are fascinating places to visit. There is always something happening. Fishing and pleasure boats glide over waters so rich in reflections that they seem to be in a magical world of their own. Fishermen mingle with visitors strolling along the quays. Seals laze in the waters. Gossiping, squabbling seabirds fly just out of reach, always watchful for the handout of a fragment of food.

The Hout Bay harbour-front emporium of Mariner's Wharf was South Africa's first. Its world-famous fish market is built around the hull of the *Kingfisher*, an original 1940s trawler from the Cape Coast fleet. At the market the delicious local delicacy called snoek and other fish are smoked daily the old-fashioned way, live lobsters crawl around in the seawater tanks, and an incredible range of seafoods is available for the kitchen. The Wharf's own special souvenir wine, in a fish-shaped bottle, is also sold, a unique memento of a visit.

Then there is the excellent Wharfside Grill Restaurant with its private dining cabins displaying fascinating relics from ocean liners such as the *Queen Mary*, ships of the Union Castle Line and the Navy. The Grill is regarded as one of Africa's top seafood restaurants. Expect to get a glimpse of the rich and famous here – it has hosted celebrities from the likes of German Chancellor Helmut Kohl and Archbishop Desmond Tutu to royalty, sportspersons and filmstars.

There are also bars serving the grogs so beloved to seafarers from the days of yore. A restaurant, right in the water's edge, is also memorable and is known for the casual seafood and the singing of sea shanties.

Batavian administration also contributed to these varied military features with a battery. The ruins of these various structures still stand. A particularly beautiful architectural survival from this period is the homestead of Kronendal farm, built in 1800 in the Cape Dutch style and now a national heritage site. It houses a restaurant.

The Hout Bay fishing industry really started around 1867 when a German immigrant, Jacob Trautman, began catching and salting snoek to export to faraway places such as Mauritius. The presence in the area of vast numbers of rock lobsters was also noticed. In 1903 the hulk of a

Above The World of Birds is a busy and fascinating refuge for over 4 000 birds and a constant flow of visitors.

British barge, wrecked at Mouille Point, was bought, towed to Hout Bay and beached. It had been converted into a processing and canning factory before being towed to Hout Bay, and it continued as a factory until 1914, when an explosion in its refrigeration chamber killed seven people. The remnants of the hulk survived until after the Second World War, when they were removed to make way for the substantial fishing harbour and two large shore factories.

A museum in the village displays interesting exhibits on the history of Hout Bay, including such early activities as manganese mining, conducted from the 1880s until 1909. The ore was sent down a chute to a jetty, part of which is still standing. Guided walks to places of natural or historical importance are organised by the museum.

The Mariner's Chest, Shell, Shipwreck and Artifact Coves are where thousands of shells, ephemera and relics of shipwrecks gathered from the world's oceans are on sale; along with handmade sea-art, marine antiques, scrimshaw, nautical books, paintings, brassware and all kinds of fascinating fishing memorabilia.

Fish and chips are, inevitably, a speciality of the area. Alfresco meals on the quayside or on the upstairs decks offer great views of the surrounding bay and a beckoning harbour. Seabirds are always in attendance, approving companions to a pleasant way of satisfying appetites aroused by the ambiance and scenic settings.

Stanley Dorman is the man who created Mariner's Wharf. Coming from a family which settled in Hout Bay in the 1890s, he was prominent in and an integral part of the Hout Bay fishing industry for over 30 years prior to establishing South Africa's first harbourfront emporium, Mariner's Wharf. The beginnings were humble: way back in the 1970s he and his wife Pam started by selling smoked snoek over weekends from a makeshift kiosk outside their small factory. .

Stanley Dorman's enthusiasm for all things related to the sea permeates the whole enterprise. In the nearby village he created a craft village, aptly named Fisherman's World, where he re-ereced and rehabilitated its old fishermen's cottages, and even character buildings such as the original post office and the old gaol. A themed section devoted to the crafts, and special skills of fisherfolk, such as net-making and shipwrighting, encompasses the lifestyle and tools of trade of a traditional coastal community. Look out for the half boat on the rocks alongside the Main Road – preserved as a landmark for prosperity, in similar style to what Stanley has done in elevating old fishing boats into the roofline at Mariner's Wharf. This is his personal tribute to the fishing families whose home has been Hout Bay for over one hundred years. Their forefathers loved the quaint harbour as a sanctuary, long before the advent of today's suburban sprawl, when the village was still a distant outpost in Cape Town's countryside. A lovely grove of historical milkwood trees has likewise been thoughtfully preserved behind the attractive Mainstream Shopping Centre.

Immediately out of Hout Bay village the marine drive reaches a junction with the road which comes down through the shady avenues of oaks from Constantia Nek. The main road veers left, bridges the course of the Hout Bay River, also known as the Disa River, makes its way through an avenue of plane trees and then reaches a junction where a short road branches off left and leads to the fishing harbour.

THE WORLD OF BIRDS
On the right-hand side of Hout Bay's Valley Road is the World of Birds wildlife sanctuary, acknowledged to be the largest bird park in Africa, and the creation of Walter Mangold.

Dedicated to wildlife, Walter Mangold acquired land in Hout Bay and began breeding birds but, in 1974, was obliged to go into liquidation. He lost his land but kept his beloved birds. With no transport except a wheelbarrow, he moved his remaining possessions, birds and cages, to the new site lose, and it took a full year of labour to get the venture going, a year spent struggling to feed the birds, to pay innumerable bills. Then one night dogs broke into the cages and killed or maimed three quarters of the birds – a devastating and almost final blow. Only the kindness of neighbours gave him the strength to continue with his dream. They erected a

Above Owls, wide-eyed and alert, represent the nightlife at World of Birds, where activity is unending.

security fence for him and in its protection he worked long days and nights building cages and creating the substantial basis of the present World of Birds.

The setting is lush. Squirrel monkeys play with visitors, delightful families of meerkats pose for photos like slightly disapproving Victorians. The birds are elegant – black swans in pensive mood, solemn secretary birds apparently talking about money and management matters in the green forest. The aviaries are so large that visitors can walk freely through them, mingling with the inmates in a landscaped garden setting. Over 3 500 birds of 450 different species, South African and exotic, can be seen there along with a community of little mammals. Many of the birds are free to come and go as they please.

VICTORIA DRIVE

The main road veers sharp right as it leaves the Hout Bay valley and climbs the slopes of the 436 m high mountain known, from pronounced similarities in shape to Lion's Head overlooking Cape Town, as Little Lion's Head. To the right there are fine views of the valley of the Hout Bay River, while silver trees and many indigenous flowering shrubs adorn the estates on either side of the road.

At its highest point the road passes over the saddle of land connecting Little Lion's Head to the Twelve Apostles (the back of Table Mountain), and an entirely new vista of sea and mountain opens up. Immediately below lies the attractive little beach and residential area of Llandudno. From Llandudno there is a short walk south to Sandy Bay, a secluded nudist beach much liked by sunbathers. The wreck of a tanker, the *Romelia*, lay on the rocks for many years after it came to grief in 1977 while being towed to a scrap-yard in the Far East. The remains now lie in deep water at the base of Sunset Rocks.

Left Sandy Bay was the Peninsula's first 'full nudist' beach, and is reached only after a long trudge through the sand.
Above The white curve of Llandudno Beach offers shelter from the wind, but the sea is cold!.
Opposite The sugarloaf shape of Little Lion's Head overlooks Llandudno and distant Hout Bay.
Overleaf The peaks of the Twelve Apostles, really a face of Table Mountain, rise behind Camps Bay.

BATHING

CAMPS BAY TO CLIFTON

The main marine drive is known as Victoria Road, for it was completed by Thomas Bain just before Queen Victoria's golden jubilee in 1887. It was a superb engineering feat by a master road builder and his last great work. Three kilometres from the Llandudno turn-off it sweeps around a bend and reveals one of the finest views of the Cape. Across a sparkling stretch of sea, Lion's Head can be seen in its most handsome aspect, with the houses of Camps Bay and Bakoven in pleasingly multicoloured disarray beneath it. The whole stretch of the Twelve Apostles provides a panorama on the right, while on the left the sea rolls in through a mass of granite boulders, with many little coves and inlets frequented by holidaymakers and fishermen.

One of these places, Hottentotshuisie ('Hottentot's shack'), developed over the years into the home of a curious community of permanent cave dwellers. Remnants of the wreck of the coaster *Bluff* lie on the rocks where it ran aground in 1965. Also on the rocks is the skeleton of the tanker *Antipolis*, wrecked in 1977 while being towed, along with the *Romelia*, to the ship-breakers.

Three kilometres along this interesting stretch of coast, the road leads past a path and stairway to the Bellsfontein kramat of the Muslim holy man Nureel Mobeen. It is said that about 13 000 Muslim slaves were buried in the protection of this sacred place, part of the original Oudekraal farm of the Van Bredas. The farmhouse is now the site of a five-star hotel.

The road enters the central suburbs of Cape Town at what is known as Bakoven ('Bake oven') from the shape of a large hollow rock on the coast. This area is now a place of bungalows built down to the water's edge, and through it Victoria Road leads directly into the suburb of Camps Bay. The place was named after Frederick von Kamptz, an invalid sailor who settled in the area in 1778. Camps Bay today is a well-to-do suburb built on the slopes of the Twelve Apostles overlooking a spacious beach, much used by sunbathers and picnickers. There is a large tidal pool and surfers find sport in a nearby cove (Glen Beach), though bathing is usually marred by very cold water and a frequent backwash. Camps Bay is the location of the attractive Theatre on the Bay.

From Camps Bay two roads lead up the slopes of the mountain, join at Kloof Nek and finally enter the city area. One of these, Geneva Drive, branches right from Victoria Road just after it passes the pavilion. The other, Kloof Road, branches right as Victoria Road leaves Camps Bay. This is a pleasant route around the slopes of Lion's Head past the Round House restaurant (an old shooting-box of the British governors), and The Glen picnic area, with fine views of Camps Bay through the trees.

Left The pocket-sized beaches of Clifton, renowned for their bikini beauties and sheltering granite boulders.

Camps Bay ends in a small headland preserved as a scenic and botanical reserve. Beyond this lie Clifton and its famous beaches (First, Second, Third and Fourth), all ideal for sunbathing and displays of feminine pulchritude, the coldness of the Atlantic Ocean providing bikini beauties with an excellent excuse not to swim. Informal (but expensive) little cottages (some not so little) are built on the cliffs overlooking the beach and are today very fashionable places in which to live. Several of these cottages were originally constructed as emergency housing after the First World War, and were regarded as temporary.

At Clifton, Lion's Head is much closer to the sea; and many of the houses along Victoria Road are built on stilts and piles. Roof-top parking is common. Before Bain made his Victoria Road, only a rough path provided a precarious way around the cliffs of what was then known as Skoenmakersgat ('Shoemaker's cave'), after a hermit who lived there and earned a living of sorts as a cobbler.

BANTRY BAY AND SEA POINT

From Clifton, Victoria Road is cut into the cliffs, winds tortuously around a mountain spur and passes through the heavily built-up area of Bantry Bay. Here, groups of apartment buildings cluster at the edge of a turbulent little bay, at the end of which is Sea Point. This suburb is crowded and unplanned with narrow, densely built-up streets. Its principal advantage is a handsome ocean front and some overwhelmingly beautiful sunsets. At the earliest opportunity a traveller should turn left out of Main Road into Beach Road, a far more relaxing route which follows the coast. An almost continuous cliff of expensive but nondescript apartment buildings lines the landward side. Sea Point has long been among Cape Town's most popular residential areas, with a vibrant night life.

Sea Point beachfront is laid out as a promenade with lawns, gardens, the Pavilion and tidal swimming-pools, including Graaff's Pool where men used to swim in the nude (the shoreline is too rocky for comfortable bathing). The pool was originally a quarry from which stone was blasted to provide ballast for the suburban railway which once connected with the city. A concrete causeway carried a trolley from the quarry to the railway line. A variety of hotels and restaurants flourish in the area. The ocean promenade is a favourite walk for people and their dogs taking the air on summer evenings.

The first building in Sea Point was a country club named the Heeren Huis ('Gentlemen's house'), erected in 1766 at the southern end. In front of the site of this long-vanished building there is an exposure of rocks of such great interest to geologists that it is marked by a plaque carrying

Right Sun-drenched Clifton is well sheltered from the summer south-easterly winds that rake the Peninsula.

the following inscription: 'The rocks between this plaque and the sea reveal an impressive contact zone of dark slate with pale intrusive granite. This interesting example of contact between sedimentary and igneous rock was first recorded by Clarke Abel in 1818. Since its discovery it has had an inspiring influence on the historical development of geology. Notable amongst those who have described it is Charles Darwin, who visited it in 1836.'

The suburb of Sea Point ends on its northeastern side at a small inlet known as Three Anchor Bay, after three anchors originally used during the Napoleonic war years to hold a defensive chain across the inlet. It is now used as a base for pleasure craft and the operations of private fishermen.

MOUILLE POINT AND GREEN POINT

From Three Anchor Bay the coast veers northwards for half a kilometre before reaching Green Point, where a lighthouse was built in 1824. From here the coast turns eastwards for a kilometre until it reaches Mouille Point, where it swings southeastwards at the beginning of the shoreline of Table Bay. It was at this point that the Dutch East India Company, between 1743 and 1746, attempted to build a *mouille* (mole or breakwater) to provide shelter for shipping in Table Bay. It was a forlorn effort – there was little money for a project which would have required massive engineering work to allow it to withstand the power of the sea.

Altogether this is a hazardous coast for shipping: misty, gale-swept and the scene of so many wrecks that a lighthouse was built in 1842 on Mouille Point to supplement the light on nearby Green Point and guide shipping entering Table Bay at night. Even with two lighthouses, however, there were still wrecks. The Mouille Point lighthouse was eventually demolished in 1908. The illumination provided by the Green Point lighthouse (often erroneously called the Mouille Point lighthouse) was increased in intensity to 850 000 candlepower and supplied with a deep-voiced foghorn.

On the southeast side of Mouille Point there is a small bay named Granger Bay, once a base for whaling. Then, in 1854, Captain Robert Granger, a merchant and shipping agent, made his home there and started a fishing industry. On a squally evening in February 1857 he saw a small schooner, the *Miner*, capsize as it was leaving Table Bay bound for Hondeklip Bay, and he rowed out alone to the distressed ship, rescuing five people. The remainder were brought to safety by another boat. The people of Cape Town paid formal tribute to Granger's gallantry. In 1964 Granger Bay became the site of the SA Merchant Navy Academy. A spec-

Left On the rocks at Bantry Bay, which was originally named Botany Bay, like the inlet in Australia.
Opposite Bantry Bay seafront under Lion's Head. A corner of Table Mountain is seen in the background.

tacular building development has converted the bay into a marina with luxurious apartments.

The coastal strip known as Mouille Point is simply what used to be called De Waterplaats ('The waterfront') of Green Point, the suburb which adjoins central Cape Town. Green Point Common is a large public area, immediately south of the Mouille Point coast and once a grazing area for the cattle of the Dutch East India Company. Here, In the 1850s the British created a horse-racing track (the grandstand was the area's first building).

Above Sea Point, where flat-dwellers enjoy a sea-front promenade past pocket beaches and tiny pools.

Today it is the site of the Metropolitan golf course, the Green Point stadium, tennis courts and athletic track. Nearby are the City Hospital and the New Somerset Hospital (which houses the Cape Medical Museum), and the Fort Wynyard, an artillery battery that protected the anchorage.

Beyond Green Point the main road enters the city area of Cape Town and our circular drive around the Cape Peninsula comes to an end 143 km from where it began at the statue of Jan van Riebeeck, at the foot of the old road named Heerengracht.

Opposite The attractions of Sea Point make it Cape Town's most densely populated suburb.

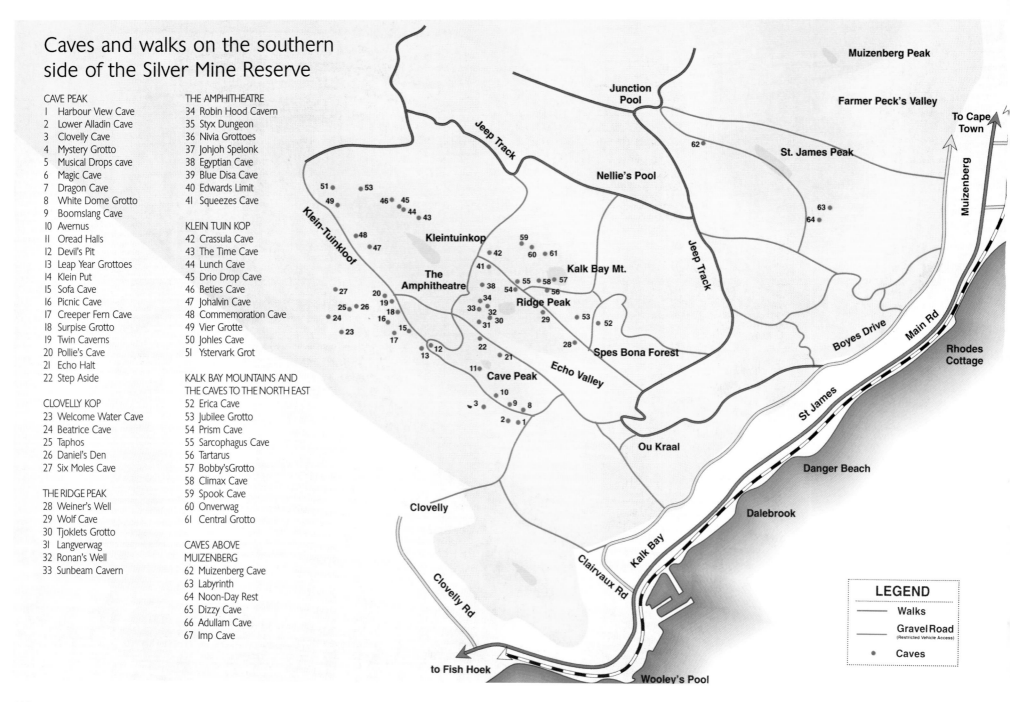

Caves and walks on the southern side of the Silver Mine Reserve

CAVE PEAK
1 Harbour View Cave
2 Lower Alladin Cave
3 Clovelly Cave
4 Mystery Grotto
5 Musical Drops cave
6 Magic Cave
7 Dragon Cave
8 White Dome Grotto
9 Boomslang Cave
10 Avernus
11 Oread Halls
12 Devil's Pit
13 Leap Year Grottoes
14 Klein Put
15 Sofa Cave
16 Picnic Cave
17 Creeper Fern Cave
18 Surpise Grotto
19 Twin Caverns
20 Pollie's Cave
21 Echo Halt
22 Step Aside

CLOVELLY KOP
23 Welcome Water Cave
24 Beatrice Cave
25 Taphos
26 Daniel's Den
27 Six Moles Cave

THE RIDGE PEAK
28 Weiner's Well
29 Wolf Cave
30 Tjoklets Grotto
31 Langverwag
32 Ronan's Well
33 Sunbeam Cavern

THE AMPHITHEATRE
34 Robin Hood Cavern
35 Styx Dungeon
36 Nivia Grottoes
37 Johjoh Spelonk
38 Egyptian Cave
39 Blue Disa Cave
40 Edwards Limit
41 Squeezes Cave

KLEIN TUIN KOP
42 Crassula Cave
43 The Time Cave
44 Lunch Cave
45 Drio Drop Cave
46 Beties Cave
47 Johalvin Cave
48 Commemoration Cave
49 Vier Grotte
50 Johles Cave
51 Ystervark Grot

KALK BAY MOUNTAINS AND THE CAVES TO THE NORTH EAST
52 Erica Cave
53 Jubilee Grotto
54 Prism Cave
55 Sarcophagus Cave
56 Tartarus
57 Bobby'sGrotto
58 Climax Cave
59 Spook Cave
60 Onverwag
61 Central Grotto

CAVES ABOVE MUIZENBERG
62 Muizenberg Cave
63 Labyrinth
64 Noon-Day Rest
65 Dizzy Cave
66 Adullam Cave
67 Imp Cave